Table of Contents

Neural Network Math: A Visual Introduction for Beginners by Michael Taylor

Published by Blue Windmill Media

© 2017 Blue Windmill Media

Blue Windmill Media

For permissions contact:

matthew@bluewindmill.co

We love reviews! Let us know your thoughts on Amazon or via email: matthew@bluewindmill.co

Cover by Blue Windmill Media

What You'll Find Inside:

200 + Easy-To-Read Images

This book is a visual introduction with over 200 images that are formatted specifically for print. This means you don't need to squint or struggle to read formulas or understand details.

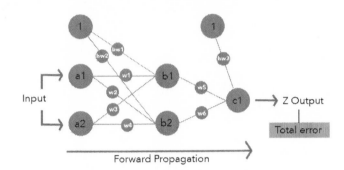

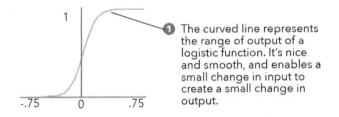

The curved line represents the range of output of a logistic function. It's nice and smooth, and enables a small change in input to create a small change in output.

What You'll Find Inside:

A Beginner-Friendly Approach

This book is designed for beginners, which is why we explain every detail line-by-line. This means that we do not gloss over definitions or assume you understand all of the elements in a formula.

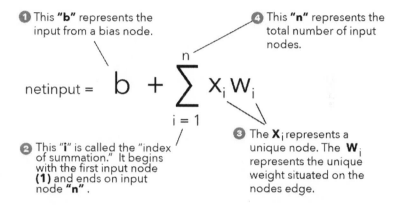

1 This **"b"** represents the input from a bias node.

4 This **"n"** represents the total number of input nodes.

$$netinput = b + \sum_{i=1}^{n} x_i w_i$$

2 This "**i**" is called the "index of summation." It begins with the first input node **(1)** and ends on input node **"n"** .

3 The X_i represents a unique node. The W_i represents the unique weight situated on the nodes edge.

$$\delta_b = (\sum_c \delta_z W_i)out_i (1 - out_i)$$

1 All of the letter **"i"'s** refer to a unique value. This value depends on the gradient we are calculating.

Don't Waste Your Time

A few points to help you make the most of this book:

1. *This book is designed as a visual introduction to neural networks. It is for BEGINNERS and those who have minimal knowledge of the topic.* If you already have a general understanding, you might not get much out of this book.

2. *You don't need to read front to back.* Skip around to what you find the most helpful or is perking your interest.

3. We *slowly* layer in new terminology and concepts each chapter. This means that if you jump to chapter 4 without having read chapter 3, you might come across terminology that you do not understand. Be aware of this, and remember: you can always jump back to clarify a topic or concept.

Part 1
Neural Networks

Ch. 1
What is a Neural Network? A Brief Overview

Neural networks have made a gigantic comeback in the last few decades and you likely make use of them everyday without realizing it, but *what exactly is* a neural network? What is it used for and how does it fit within the broader arena of machine learning?

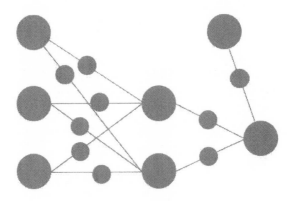

A Basic Neural Network

In this chapter we are going to gently explore these topics so that we can be prepared to dive deep further on. To start, we'll begin with a high-level overview of machine learning and then drill down into the specifics of a neural network.

Machine Learning

Machine learning is the science of getting computers to act without being explicitly programmed, and it is our biggest step towards making artificial intelligence a reality. If you like movies, think *Ex Machina* or *Transcendence* or *I, Robot* - but just the good parts! Machine learning is a field within computer science that has gained incredible traction within the last few decades and it likely touches your life everyday.

From Google search to Uber rides and YouTube ads, machine learning is not only a buzzword but also increasingly being tested and used in countless industries to improve speed, reduce errors and boost efficiency.

Machine learning is all about algorithms - or rules - that are used to work with data and make predictions. For example, email providers such as *Yahoo!* and *Gmail* use algorithms to filter your email and keep spam out of your inbox.

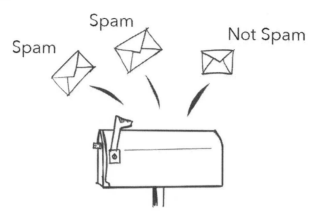

On a high-level, spam filtering algorithms achieve this by being trained on what *is spam* and *is not spam*. For this to happen, the algorithm is fed thousands of emails labelled as spam and not spam, and after analyzing each email, the algorithm eventually "learns" how to spot spam by identifying common characteristics that separate it from legitimate, real email. These characteristics could be certain phrases or words, such as "earn per week", "no strings attached" or even "vacation".

There are many types of machine learning algorithms that are currently used, and there are a variety of ways they can be categorized. One of the easiest to understand is grouping by similarity and learning style.

Similarity:

Similarity	Algorithm Ex #1	Algorithm Ex #2
Regression	Logisitc Regression	Linear Regression
Decision Tree	CART	ID3
Clustering	Naive Bayes	Gaussian Naive Bayes
Neural Networks	Back Propagation	Convolutional (CNN)

* This list is not comprehensive. There are many more algorithms and similarity categories.

Learning Style

On a high level, there are three popular ways that machine learning can be approached:

#1: Supervised Learning

With supervised learning, the learning algorithm is presented with a set of inputs along with their desired outputs (also called labels). The goal is to discover a rule that enables the computer to re-create the outputs, or in other words, *map* the input to output.

For example, think of categorizing images of cats and dogs. To teach an algorithm what a dog is and a cat is, an algorithm would be presented with thousands of images of each, and each image would be labelled as "dog" or "cat".

Image   Label

This label is the desired output for each image, and by analyzing each example the algorithm would eventually be able to classify new images of cats and dogs with very minimal error. *In reality this label is not a written word such as "Dog" or "Cat", but a numerical representation of each label. We'll dive more into this further on.

#2: Unsupervised Learning

With unsupervised learning, an algorithm is presented with a set of inputs but *no desired outputs*, which means the algorithm must find structure and patterns *on its own*. To link this to the supervised example above, if images of dogs and cats were fed into an unsupervised algorithm, each image would not have a label that identifies it as a "cat" or "dog".

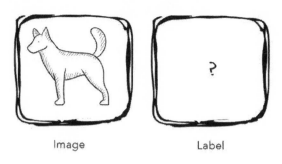

Image   Label

Instead, the algorithm would have to find patterns on its own as it assess the thousands of dog and cat images. Patterns could be the length of the animal, height, etc.

#3 Semi-Supervised Learning

Semi-supervised learning (SSL) is a mixture of the previous two learning styles, which means it is fed a combination of labelled and unlabelled inputs. Practically speaking, this means that SSL algorithms must find structure and patterns on their own but do have some help from labelled inputs.

A great example is web page classification into categories such as "shopping" or "news". It would be extremely expensive and time-consuming to hire a team to manually label thousands of websites, but an alternative does exist: labelling a small subset of websites. With SSL, this small subset would be fed into an algorithm as the "labelled" set alongside thousands of other websites that are not labelled. The algorithm could be trained on the unlabeled set first before being fine-tuned with the labelled set.

Neural Networks

A neural network, also known as an artificial neural network, is a type of machine learning algorithm that is inspired by the biological brain. It is one of many popular algorithms that is used within the world of machine learning, and its goal is to solve problems in a similar way to the human brain.

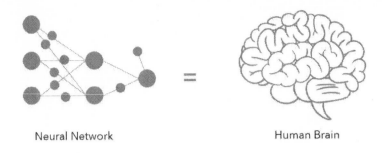

Neural Network   Human Brain

Neural networks are part of what's called Deep Learning, which is a branch of machine learning that has proved valuable for solving difficult problems, such as recognizing things in images and language processing.

Neural networks take a different approach to problem solving than that of conventional computer programs. To solve a problem, conventional software uses an algorithmic approach, i.e. the computer follows a set of instructions in order to solve a problem.

In contrast, neural networks approach problems in a very different way by trying to mimic how neurons in the human brain work. In fact, they learn by example rather than being programmed to perform a specific task.

Technically, they are composed of a large number of highly interconnected processing elements (nodes) that work in parallel to solve a specific problem, which is similar to how the human brain works.

Now, there is a lot that can be said about neural networks, but since this is an overview, here are the top 5 things you should know:

#1. Neural Networks Are Specific
Neural networks are always built to solve a specific type of problem, although this doesn't mean they can be used as "general purpose" tools. For example, you will not find a "general purpose" algorithm that you can sink data into for prediction or estimation...at least not yet!

Examples of specific uses include:
- Prediction
- Forecasting
- Classification
- Pattern recognition

Real world examples include: Stock market prediction, real estate appraisal, medical diagnosis, handwriting recognition, and recognizing images.

#2. Neural Networks Have 3 Basic Parts:

A neural network has three basic sections, or parts, and each part is composed of "nodes".

1. Input Layer
2. Hidden Layer(s)
3. Output Layer

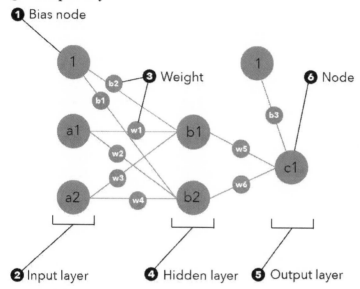

#3. Neural Networks Are Built 2 Ways

On a high level, neural networks can be built two ways:

1. **Feedforward:** With a feedforward neural network, signals travel only one way, from input to output. These types of networks are more straightforward and used extensively in pattern recognition. A convolutional neural network (CNN or ConvNet) is a specific type of feedforward network that is often used in image recognition.

2. **Feedback (or recurrent neural networks, RNNs):** With an RNN, signals can travel both directions and there can be loops. Feedback networks are more powerful and complex than CNNs, and they are always changing. Despite this, RNNs have been less influential than feedforward networks, in part because the learning algorithms for recurrent nets are (at least to date) less

powerful. However, RNNs are still extremely interesting and are much closer in spirit to how our brains work than feedforward networks.

#4. Neural Networks Are Either Fixed or Adaptive

Neural networks can be either fixed or adaptive.

1. **Fixed**: The weight values in a fixed network remain static. They do not change.
2. **Adaptive**: The weight values in an adaptive network are not static and can change.

#5. Neural Networks Use 3 Types of DataSets

Neural networks are often built and trained using three datasets:

- **Training dataset:** The training dataset is used to adjust the weights of the neural network.
- **Validation dataset:** The validation dataset is used to minimize a problem known as overfitting, which we will cover in more detail.
- **Testing dataset:** The testing dataset is used as a final test to gauge how accurately the network has been trained.

These three sets are usually taken from one very large dataset that represents the "gold standard" of data for a project, and are often split 60/20/20:

Training data: 60%
Validation data: 20%
Testing data: 20%.

EVERYBODY JUST WANTS *to be* LOVED

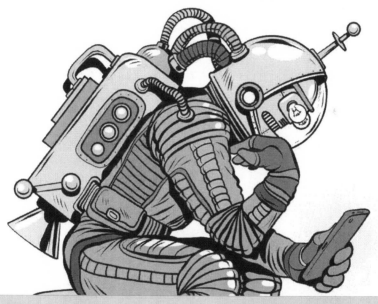

Show Astro Robot some love and
DROP US AN EMAIL
or
LEAVE A REVIEW
and let us know how we did!

Part 2
The Math of Neural Networks

The Math of Neural Networks: Introduction

There are many reasons why neural networks fascinate us and have captivated headlines in recent years. They make web searches better, organize photos, and are even used in speech translation. Heck, they can even generate encryption. At the same time, they are also mysterious and mind-bending: how exactly do they accomplish these things ? What goes on *inside* a neural network?

On a high level, a network learns just like we do, through trial and error. Once we dig a bit deeper though, we discover that a handful of mathematical functions play a major role in the trial and error process. It also becomes clear that a grasp of the underlying mathematics helps clarify *how a network learns.*

This is why the following chapters will be devoted to understanding the mathematics that drive a neural network. To do this, we will use a feedforward network as our model and follow input as it moves through the network.

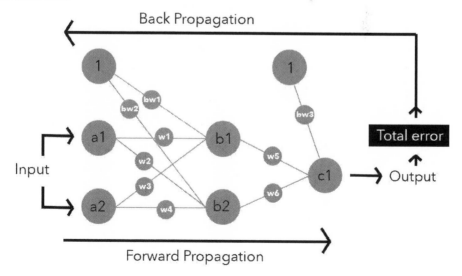

This "process" of moving through the network is complex though, so to make it easier and bite-size, we will divide it into 5 stages and take it slow.

Each of the stages includes at least one mathematical function, and we will devote an entire chapter to every stage. Our goal is that by the end, you will find neural networks less mind-bending and simply more fascinating. What's more, we hope that you'll be able to confidently explain these concepts to others and make use of them for yourself.

Here are the stages we will be exploring:

Stage 1: Forward Propagation
Required: Summation operator
Required: Activation function

Stage 2: Calculate the Total Error
Required: Cost function

Stage 3: Calculate the Gradients
Required: Partial derivative
Required: Chain Rule

Stage 4: Gradient Checking
Required: Gradient checking formula

Stage 5: Updating Weights
Required: Weight update formula

However, before diving into the stages, we are going to clarify the terminology and notation that we will be using. We will also take a moment to build on the topics and ideas introduced in the previous chapters. Accomplishing these things will build up a solid framework and provide us with the tools required to move forward.

A extra few words before moving on:
You might be scratching your head and wondering if all networks have the same mathematical functions. The answer is a loud *no*, and for a few good reasons, including the network architecture, its purpose, and even the personal preferences of its developer. However, there is a general framework for feedforward models that includes a handful of mathematical functions, which is what we will be investigating.

On another note, the following chapters require a college-level grasp of algebra, statistics and calculus. A major concept you'll come across is calculating partial derivatives, which itself makes use of the chain rule. Please be aware of this! If you are rusty in these areas you might find yourself repeatedly frustrated. The Khan Academy offers top-notch free courses in algebra, calculus and statistics. Visit the Khan Academy at https://www.khanacademy.org/.

Ch. 3

Terminology and Notation

If you are new to the field of neural networks or machine learning in general, one of the most confusing aspects can be the terminology and notation used. Textbooks, online lectures, and papers often vary in this regard.

To help minimize potential frustration we have put together a few charts to explain what you can expect in this book.

The first is a list of common terms used to describe the same function, object or action, along with a clarification of which term we will be using. The second list contains common notation, along with a clarification of the notation we will be using. Hopefully this helps!

Note: The majority of these terms will be explained throughout each stage. However, you can always take a peek at our extended definitions section for additional help.

Terms:

Term	We Will be Using
Activation Function / Transfer Function	Activation Function
Artificial Neural Network / Neural Network	Neural Network
Learning Algorithm / Learning Rule	Learning Algorithm
Node / Neuron	Node
Synapse / Edge / Connection	Edge
Target / Taret Output / Ideal Output / Desired Output / Target Pattern	Target Output

The notation chart is below. You might find it helpful to bookmark the page for reference.

Notation	Common Usage	We Will be Using
x	Denotes network input. Ex: $x_1, x_2, x_3, \ldots x_n$	The letter **a**. Ex: $a_1, a_2, a_3, \ldots a_n$
$\hat{y}$ or z	Denotes total network output.	z
n or m	Denotes number of training examples.	n
$\sigma(x)$ or $\phi(x)$	Denotes the logistic activation function, which computes the output of a node.	On a high level, we will use $\sigma(x)$. When computing partial derivatives, we will use the syntax **outb1,** where b1 is the node we are calculating the output for.
$J(W)$ or $J(\theta)$	Denotes the cost function, which is the total error of the network.	On a high level we will use the phrase **total error**. We will also use a capital **E** when calculating partial derivatives.
$\sum$	Denotes the summation operator, which computes the net input of a node.	On a high level we will use $\sum$. When computing partial derivatives we will use the syntax **netb1,** were b1 is the node we are calculating the input for.
η	Denotes the learning rate.	η
$W_{ji}^{(1)}$	Denotes a weight in the first layer going from input **i** to hidden **j**.	We will refer to weights with numbers. Ex: W_5
t_i and z_i	Denotes the target and actual output of a single output node.	t_i and z_i
θ_w	Denotes a specific weight within a vector.	θ_w

Ch. 4

Pre-Stage: Creating the Network Structure

In the previous chapters, we touched on a variety of neural network architectures such as CNNs and RNNs. Although each is slightly different, all have a structure - or shell - that is made up of similar parts. These parts are called *hyperparameters*, and include elements such as the number of layers, nodes and the learning rate.

Hyperparameters are essentially fine tuning knobs that can be tweaked to help a network successfully train. In fact, they are determined before a network trains, and can only be adjusted manually by the individual or team who created the network. The network itself does not adjust them.

You can see some of these hyperparameters in the feedforward network below:

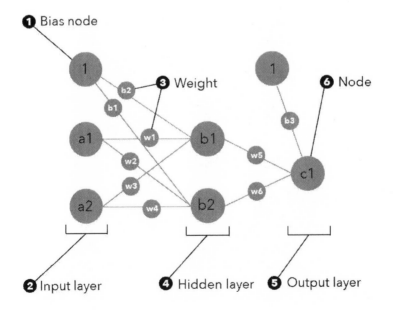

In this chapter we are going to take a brief pause to explore these hyperparameters because they are extremely important. Not only are they tuning knobs that help a network train, but all of a networks mathematical calculations depend on them being in place. We will begin by defining the two categories of hyperparameters, and then briefly explore each.

Types of Hyperparameters

Broadly speaking there are two categories of hyperparameters: required and optional.

Required Hyperparameters Include:

- Total number of input nodes
- Total number of hidden layers
- Total number of hidden nodes in each hidden layer
- Total number of output nodes
- Weight values
- Bias values
- Learning Rate

Optional Hyperparameters Include:*

- Learning rate schedule (a.k.a learning rate decay)
- Momentum
- Mini-batch size
- Weight decay
- Dropout

*This list is not exhaustive !

Now, let's take a brief look at each of the required hyperparameters. Please note that many new terms will be introduced below, and we will explain each as we move throughout the stages.

Input Node

An input node contains the *input* of the network and this input is *always* numerical. If the input is not numerical by default, it is always converted. For example:

- Images are often converted to grayscale, and each pixel is measured on a scale of 0 to 1 for intensity (where 0 (zero) is black, and 1 is white).
- Text is converted to numbers. For example, male/female might be converted to 1 and 0 (zero), respectively.
- Sound is converted to numbers that represent amplitude across time, with 0 (zero) when silent and 1 when loud.
-

An input node is located within the input layer, which is the first layer of a neural network. Each input node represents a single *dimension* and is often called a *feature,* and all features are stored within a *vector.*

For example, if you have an image of 16x16 pixels as input, you have a total of 256 input nodes. This is because each input node represents a single image pixel, and there are 256 pixels in total (16x16).

Now, in light of the descriptive language available, there are multiple ways an input vector can be described, including:
- 256 nodes
- 256 features
- 256 dimensions

The terminology can be quite heavy, so we will keep to using *node* in this book!

Hidden Layer

A hidden layer is a layer of nodes between the input and output layers. There can be either a single hidden layer or multiple hidden layers in a network, and the more that exist, the "deeper" the learning that a network can perform. In fact, multiple hidden layers are what the term *deep learning* refers to. Selecting the number of hidden layers is a complex topic and beyond the scope of our overview.

Hidden Node

A hidden node is a node within a hidden layer. A hidden layer can have *many hidden* nodes, and there are various theories for implementing the correct amount. General rules of thumb coupled with trial and error are what guide most data scientists and programmers. Studies have demonstrated that layers which contain the same amount of nodes generally performed the same *or better* than a decreasing *or* increasing pyramid shaped network. We won't go any deeper than that!

Output Node

An output node is a node within an output layer. There can be a single or multiple output nodes depending on the objective of the network. For example, if a network exists to classify handwritten digits from 0 to 9, there would be 10 output nodes (0 (zero) is one of them, hence there are 10 output nodes). Similar to the input of a network, the output is a *vector*.

Weight Value

A weight is a variable that sits on an *edge* between nodes. The output of every node in a layer is multiplied by a weight, then summed with other weighted nodes in that layer to become the *net input* of a node in the following layer. Weights are important because they are the primary *tuning knob* that is used to train a network.

Algorithms are typically used to assign random weights for a neural network. A popular range is between -1 and 1.

Bias Value

A bias node is an extra node added to each hidden and output layer, and it connects to every node within each respective layer. A bias is never connected to a previous layer, but is simply added to the input of a layer. In addition, it typically has a constant value of 1 or -1 and has a weight on its connecting edge.

Technically, the bias provides every node in a neural network with a trainable constant value (1 or -1). On a practical level, this enables the activation function to be shifted to the left or right. Alongside the adjusting of weights, this "shifting" can be very important and critical for successful learning. We will cover activation functions in more detail later on!

Below is an example of the Logistic (Sigmoid) activation function plotted on a graph. It is a fantastic visualization of how a bias can help "shift" the output of a node, and ultimately help a network successfully train.

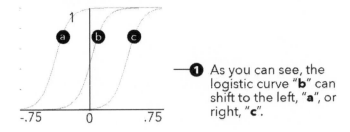

1 As you can see, the logistic curve "**b**" can shift to the left, "**a**", or right, "**c**".

Learning Rate

The learning rate is a value that speeds up or slows down how quickly an algorithm learns. Technically, it determines the size of step an algorithm takes when moving towards a *global minimum,* i.e., the lowest error rate. *Although in practice, the global minimum is often not reached and the algorithm settles for a local minimum that is close to the global.

A learning rate can be static and remain consistent throughout the learning process, or it can be programmed to scale down as the network's error rate falls. A few more points to consider:

- There are multiple theories on how to select a proper learning rate, but in most cases selection will depend on trial and error.
- A learning rate that is too high can impact a networks ability to converge - or in other words, it will fail to reach a *global minimum.* It can also cause the network to overshoot and/or diverge. See below for an example of what divergence looks like. Note that with divergence, the lowest point (bottom of "U" shaped surface) is never reached. Instead, the network "bounces" around and never reaches the bottom.

1 Diverging can occur when the learning rate is too large.

- A learning rate that is too low can cause a network to take a *long time* to converge.

Most study cases you will find online make use of learning rates close to o (zero), such as 0.1.

Momentum

Momentum is a value that is used to help push a network out of a *local minimum,* which is a false "lowest-error" that networks often become trapped in. Technically, momentum must be predetermined for the network, and is also one of the most popular techniques added to backpropagation. Momentum and backpropagation will be discussed in detail further on.

Now onto Stage 1.

Stage 1: Forward Propagation

Now that we understand the structure of a neural network, we can investigate how input *moves* through the network to become output. This process is technically called *forward propagation*.

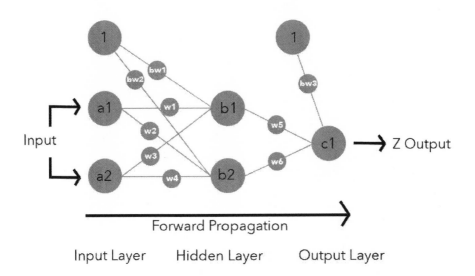

When input is passed into the network, it moves from one layer to the next until it passes through the output layer. A total of two mathematical functions are repeatedly used to make all of this possible, and we will examine both in this chapter.

This stage is organized into three parts.
1. Understanding The Mathematical Functions Used
2. Understanding Matrices
3. Fitting it All Together: Review

Ch. 5
Understanding the Mathematical Functions Used

There are a total of two mathematical functions used in this stage, and both of these functions occur *inside of* every hidden and output node. Yes, you heard right: every single node! These functions include:

- Summation operator
- Activation function

A fantastic way to understand how and where these functions operate is to view them as a *working pair* within each node:

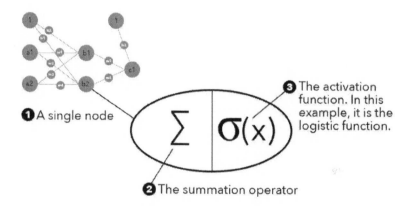

① A single node

② The summation operator

③ The activation function. In this example, it is the logistic function.

What is a Summation Operator?
The summation operator sums a sequence of numbers, and is a convenient tool to use when dealing with large number sets and/or the repetition of an operation (such as addition or multiplication).

Within a neural network, the summation operator sums all of a node's inputs to create a *net input*. Below is the operator in its general form, followed by its specific usage for calculating the net input of a node.

General Summation Operator

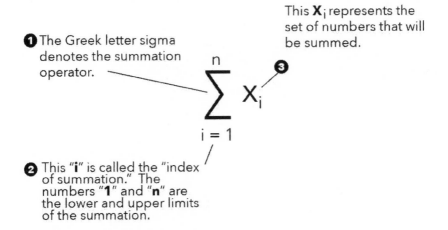

❶ The Greek letter sigma denotes the summation operator.

This X_i represents the set of numbers that will be summed.

$$\sum_{i=1}^{n} X_i$$

❸

❷ This "**i**" is called the "index of summation." The numbers "**1**" and "**n**" are the lower and upper limits of the summation.

Forward Propagation: Summation Operator

When it comes to calculating the net input of a node, the summation operator looks as follows:

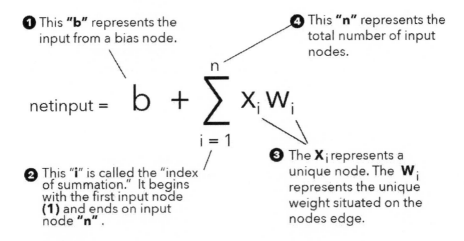

❶ This "**b**" represents the input from a bias node.

❹ This "**n**" represents the total number of input nodes.

$$netinput = b + \sum_{i=1}^{n} X_i W_i$$

❷ This "**i**" is called the "index of summation." It begins with the first input node (**1**) and ends on input node "**n**".

❸ The X_i represents a unique node. The W_i represents the unique weight situated on the nodes edge.

A Few Points to Consider :

The Bias:

The bias value is typically set to 1. Since a bias does not have an input that can alter this value, the output of a bias is always 1. This output of 1 is then multiplied by the bias' edge weight to become input for a node. Therefore, the final output of a bias to a node is typically its edge weight value.

Input and Input Node:
The terms **"input"** and **"input node"** in this formula do not refer specifically to the net input of the network. They simply refer to the input into any hidden or output layer node. Therefore, this formula can be applied to a node in any hidden or output layer.

The summation operator is used in conjunction with matrices, and therefore an example of how this works will be given when matrices are discussed in Stage 1.

Why is a Summation Operator Used ?
Each hidden node and output node in a neural network has multiple input values. For these input values to successfully move through the network and create an output, they must be summed and turned into a *single value* when entering a new node - and this is exactly what the summation function does. To do this, the summation operator makes use of **matrices**, and its output is typically called a **dot product** or **inner product**.

What is an Activation Function?
Within a neural network, an activation function receives the output of the summation operator and transforms it into the final output of a node. On a high level, an activation function essentially "squashes" the input and transforms it into an output value that represents how much a node should contribute (i.e., how much a node should fire).

As an example, below you can see the graph of the **logistic activation function (also called Sigmoid)**, which squashes its input to create output between 0 (zero) and 1:

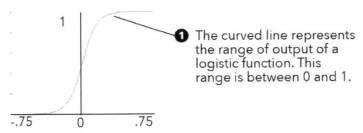

1

-.75   0   .75

① The curved line represents the range of output of a logistic function. This range is between 0 and 1.

The equation for an activation function differs between functions. Below is the equation for the Logistic activation function that we graphed above:

$$f(x) = \frac{1}{1 + e^{-x}}$$

② This **"x"** is the net input to a particular node.

① This **"e"** stands for a mathematical constant that is approximately equal to 2.71828.

Types of Activation Functions

There are many types of activation functions to choose from, and a single network will often make use of multiple types. For example, a network might use the logistic function for the hidden layer nodes but use a different function for the output nodes, such as the softmax function. This is because functions differ in output, and also have unique strengths and weaknesses.

Below is a list of various activations functions. It is not an exhaustive list, but it is helpful !

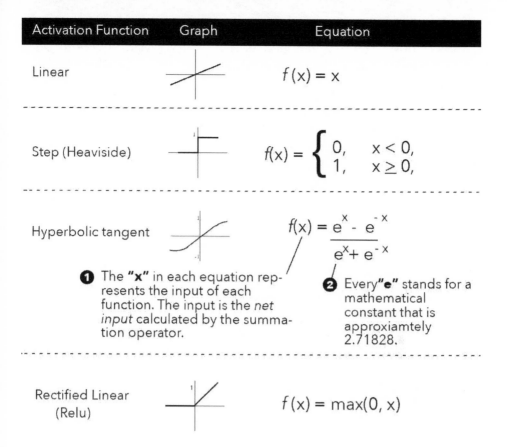

Activation Function	Graph	Equation
Linear		$f(x) = x$
Step (Heaviside)		$f(x) = \begin{cases} 0, & x < 0, \\ 1, & x \geq 0, \end{cases}$
Hyperbolic tangent		$f(x) = \dfrac{e^x - e^{-x}}{e^x + e^{-x}}$

❶ The "**x**" in each equation represents the input of each function. The input is the *net input* calculated by the summation operator.

❷ Every "**e**" stands for a mathematical constant that is approxiamtely 2.71828.

| Rectified Linear (Relu) | | $f(x) = \max(0, x)$ |

Let's pause for a moment and look at the functions above.

With the **linear function**, you can see that the input *is* the output. There is no transformation that occurs. *F(x)* is simply *x*.

Now, contrast the linear function with the **step (heaviside) function**. With a step function, the output is either 0 (zero) or 1. You can see that if **x** is less than zero, the output is zero. If **x** is greater than zero or equal to zero, the output is 1. Hence, the function forms a *step* from zero to 1 when graphed.

Next, we have the **hyperbolic tangent function (tanh)**. This function is very similar to the logistic function, except that its output is between -1 and 1. This flexible range of output is exactly what enables both the logistic and tanh functions to solve nonlinear problems (we'll dive into this more below).

Finally, we come to the **rectified linear unit (ReLU)** function. With this function, all input that is <= 0 (zero) is set to 0 (zero). All input that is > 0 (zero) is equal to the input.

Why is an Activation Function Used ?

As stated above, activation functions are used to transform the output of a summation operator into the final output of a node. In recent years (2015 -) the ReLU function has gained popularity because of its phenomenal performance within deep neural networks, especially for image recognition with convolutional neural networks (CNNs).

There are multiple theories as to why its performance is superior, but no consensus has been reached.

Logistic and Hyperbolic Activation Functions

Apart from the ReLU function, the logistic and tanh functions are also popular. You will see these functions widely used in tutorials and lectures online, especially outside of CNNs.

Let's dig a bit deeper though. Why exactly are the logistic and tanh functions so popular? Here are two reasons why.

Reason #1: Introducing Non-Linearity. Neural networks are often used to solve nonlinear problems, i.e. problems that cannot be solved by separating classes with a straight line. Image classification is an excellent example of this.

An example of the importance of non-linearity can be seen below. With the image on the left, there are two groups that are being classified. These groups are easily separated with a straight line, and thus can be solved linearly.

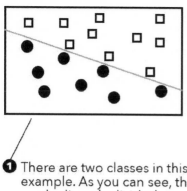 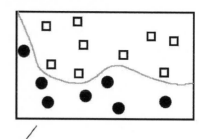

1 There are two classes in this example. As you can see, they can be linearly divided.

2 There are two classes in this example, but they cannot be divided linearly. Non-linearity must be introduced into the problem to successfully classify. The logistic (Sigmoid) and tanh functions both introduce this, and when used in conjunction with a multi-layer neural network can solve these problems.

Activation functions such as the tanh and logistic essentially "break" the linearity of a network and enable it to solve more complex problems. This act of breaking is an essential component that enables networks to *map* the input of a network to the output of a network and successfully train.

Reason #2: Limiting output. The tanh and logistic functions limit the output of a node to a certain range.

Ranges:
1. The Hyperbolic Tangent function produces output between -1 and 1.
2. The Logistic function produces output between 0 and 1.

There are numerous benefits to limiting output over these ranges, and one of the most significant is weight adjustment.

As you saw earlier in the activation function chart , both the logistic and tanh functions are curved. This curve, or smoothness, represents the type of output that either function can produce. On a practical level, the smoothness enables small changes in the weights and bias to produce a small change in the output.

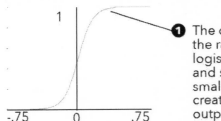

1. The curved line represents the range of output of a logistic function. It's nice and smooth, and enables a small change in input to create a small change in output.

You can view this as fine tuning that makes the task of "learning" much smoother and easier.

Now, take a moment and contrast this with the **step function**, which is...for lack of a better explanation, similar to a step.

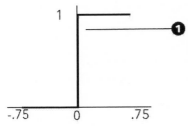

1. The **bolded** step represents the range of output for a Step (Heaviside) function. All output is either 0 (zero) or 1. A small change in input can create a large change in output.

The step function produces an output of either 1 or 0, but nothing in-between those numbers. This means that a small change in a weight or bias is not reflected by a small change in output. Instead, the output might possibly switch from 0 (zero) to 1, or vice versa. There is no range, and this can make learning difficult!

Ch. 6
Understanding Matrices: A Brief Overview

Forward propagation is a repetitive task that requires repeated calculation using the functions we introduced above. Imagine calculating the input and output for a large network with hundreds or thousands of nodes - and by hand! The amount of time this would entail is ridiculous and impractical. Plus, the likelihood of an error would be extremely high. No thanks!

Matrices provide us with a tidy, fast and extremely useful shortcut for calculating large amounts of data in both forward and backpropagation. This section will touch on both uses, although backpropagation will be discussed further in Stage 3 and onward.

In reality, pushing matrix multiplication to its limits is one of the reasons why neural networks are powerful and useful. So let's take a moment to understand them!

What is a Matrix ?

A matrix is a rectangular array of numbers written between two square brackets. On a very high level, this can be thought of as the rows and columns in a spreadsheet. For example, the illustration below contains two dimensions - 2 rows and 4 columns, and would be labelled as a "2 by 4" matrix.

A 2 by 4 Matrix ☆

File   Edit   View   Insert   Format   Data   Tools   Add-ons   H

🖨 ↶ ↷ 🖌 $ % .0 .00 123 ▾   Arial   ▾   10

ƒx

	A	B	C	D
1	90	85	92	97
2	100	77	67	81
3				
4				
5				

On a technical level, a matrix is a two-dimensional array. An array is a one-dimensional list of data that can include numbers, strings etc. What's more, each element in the list is assigned a position *within* the list.

For example:

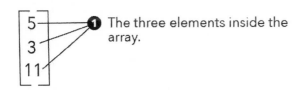

❶ The three elements inside the array.

Now, one of the items in the array above *can actually be an array* - basically an array of arrays, and this is what a matrix is.

For example:

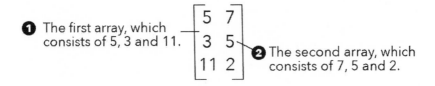

❶ The first array, which consists of 5, 3 and 11.

❷ The second array, which consists of 7, 5 and 2.

How Are The Entries in a Matrix Referenced ?

The entries in a matrix are typically referred to using numbers that denote the row and column. It's fairly straightforward.

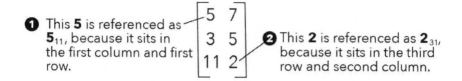

① This **5** is referenced as **5**$_{11}$, because it sits in the first column and first row.

② This **2** is referenced as **2**$_{31}$, because it sits in the third row and second column.

For example, in the above matrix the top lefthand **5** would be referenced as **5**$_{11}$ because it sits in the first row and first column. Likewise, the **2** would be referenced as **2**$_{31}$ because it sits in the third row and second column. As a whole, this matrix would be referred to as a 3 x 2 matrix, since it is 3 rows by 2 columns.

What Type of Data Does a Matrix Contain?

Think of all the information that flows through a network - both forwards and backwards. This information is stored in either a vector or matrix as it moves throughout the network.

Information stored in a matrix:
- Weights

Information stored in a vector:
- Input features
- Node inputs
- Node outputs
- Network error (which essentially is a list of weight gradients)
- Biases

How Are Matrices Used?

Matrices are used for every major calculation in both forward and backpropagation. To illustrate this, we will analyze how inputs are moved to the first hidden layer.

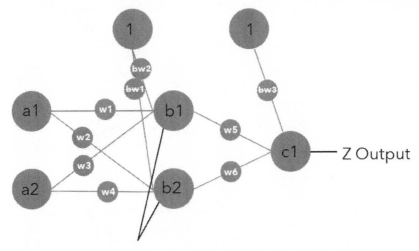

① To calculate the net input of **b1** and **b2**, we need to multiply **a1** and **a2** by their respective weights and then sum the answers into **b1** and **b2**, respectively. The bias also needs to be added.

To calculate the input into nodes **b1** and **b2**, we need to multiply all of the inputs into each node by their respective weights. This includes the bias value. For this to happen, the network input (which is a vector) is multiplied by the matrix of weight values that sits between *it* and the hidden layer.

To make this clearer, below is another visual example. The example is greatly simplified and should make this concept easier to grasp.

In the example above, the input vector would be multiplied by the weight matrix and the result would be added to a bias to create a new *vector* - which would be the net input to **node b1.** Let's perform this calculation below.

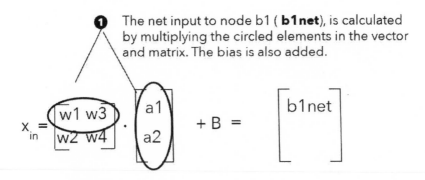

① The net input to node b1 (**b1net**), is calculated by multiplying the circled elements in the vector and matrix. The bias is also added.

To calculate **b1net** (the input to node b1), we simply need to multiply each output from **a1** and **a2** by their respective weights and then add the bias. Remember, the bias **B** is the result of the bias value multiplied by its corresponding edge weight.

Notice that we *always begin* at the top of the vector and move *horizontally* across each row in the matrix. By doing this, we multiply each element in the vector by each element in a *single* matrix row. Take a look back at the network layout above if this is not clear.

If we wrote this out:

b1net = (a1 * w1) + (a2 * w3) + bias

To clarify, the bias is arrived at by multiplying the bias value * bias weight. Thus, the above can be broken down even further:

b1net = (a1 * w1) + (a2 * w3) + (bias * bw1)

And since the bias value is typically **"1"**, this can be finalized as:

b1net = (a1 * w1) + (a2 * w3) + (1 * bw1)

The exact same process is followed for calculating the net input for b2.

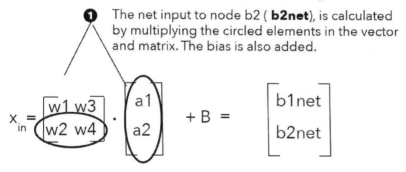

1 The net input to node b2 (**b2net**), is calculated by multiplying the circled elements in the vector and matrix. The bias is also added.

And written out:

b2net = (a1 * w2) + (a2 * w4) + bias

Again, the above can be pulled apart further to demonstrate how the bias is arrived at:

b2net = (a1 * w2) + (a2 * w4) + (1 * bw2)

Ch. 7
Fitting it All Together: A Review

In this stage we learned about how input is moved through a network to become output. Each input node is called a *feature*, and together, all features are stored in a *vector*. The information within the vector is moved through the network using two mathematical functions: the summation operator and activation function.

The summation operator sums all of the inputs into a node to create the *net input*. The activation function takes the *net input* and creates the final output of the node. Both mathematical functions occur within every hidden layer node and output layer node.

We also learned that matrix and vector multiplication are used to speed the entire process up and reduce errors.

Big Picture
Below is an illustration that highlights the *big picture* of this stage. Moving from left to right, you can see the following:

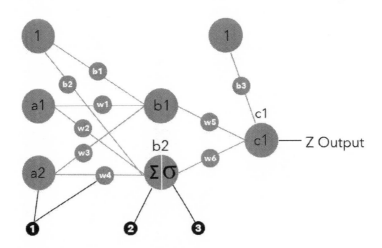

Step 1: Each input is multiplied by a weight as it travels over an *edge* (connecting line) to a node in a following layer.
Step 2: All inputs to a node, including the bias, are summed using the *summation operator*. The result is called the *total net input*.

Step 3: The *total net input* is then fed into an *activation function*, which transforms the net input into a new output. This new output is then sent out over one or more edges and multiplied by a weight, and the cycle continues until the output layer calculations are completed.

Stage 2: Calculating The Total Error

Things are looking good! We have successfully moved our input through the neural network. Our next step is to compute the *total error* of the network, which will enable the network to adjust its weights and *learn*. The total error is the difference between a network's *actual output* and *target output*.

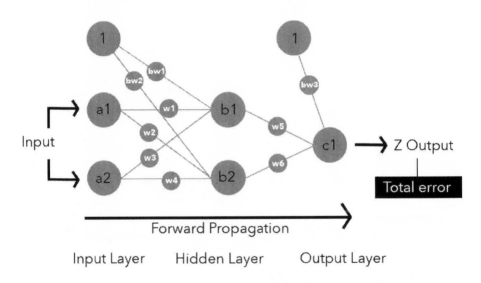

Forward Propagation

Input Layer   Hidden Layer   Output Layer

In supervised learning, each input has a corresponding target output, and this target output is what the network is aiming to replicate. In the example below, the image of a chicken has a target vector that the network will compare with the network's actual output - and any difference is labelled as the network's *total error.*

The process of matching the actual output to the target output is technically called *mapping*, and we will learn more about this moving forward. A single mathematical function is used to calculate the total error.

This stage is organized into three parts:
1. Forward
2. Understanding The Mathematical Functions Used
3. Fitting it All Together: Review

Part 1: Forward

Depending on where the network is in the training process, this stage could be the final stage. It will, however, *always be the final stage for any network that successfully trains.*

Once this stage is completed and the total error is calculated, two things can happen:

1. The network has successfully converged, ie., it has reached an acceptable low error and reached a *global minimum* or an acceptable *local minimum* that is close enough to the *global minimum*. At this point, the network ceases training.
2. The network has failed to converge. In this case, a *minimum* has not been discovered, and the network continues on to Stage 3 and continues to train. This process repeats itself until the network has converged.

Part 2: Mathematical Functions

There is a single mathematical function used in this stage, and it is only used once during forward propagation when it is applied to the output of a neural network.

- Cost Function (also referred to as a *loss function or error function*)

What is a Cost Function?

Within a neural network, a cost function transforms everything that occurs within the network into a number that represents the *total error* of the network. Essentially, it is a measure of how *wrong* a network is. On a more technical level, it maps an event or values of one or more variables onto a real number. This real number represents a "cost" or "loss" associated with the event or values.

Types of Cost Functions

There are many types of cost functions to choose from. Popular options include the Mean Squared Error, Squared Error, Root Mean Square Error and Sum of Square Errors (reasons for this will be elaborated on in the next sub-section). Other cost functions include Cross-Entropy, Exponential, Hellinger Distance, and the Kullback–Leibler Divergence.

We won't dive into every cost function, but let's pause to examine the first three.

1.Mean Squared Error (MSE).

The Mean Squared Error function takes the sum of all squared output errors in a network and averages them. In other words, the MSE measures the difference between the target output and actual output of training examples in a network.

1.The MSE equation is as follows

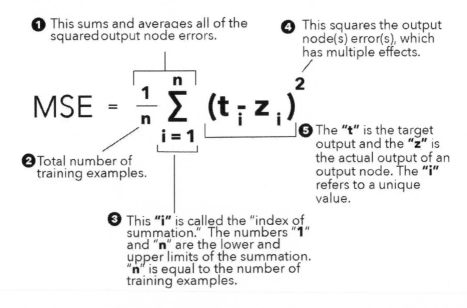

❶ This sums and averages all of the squared output node errors.

❹ This squares the output node(s) error(s), which has multiple effects.

$$MSE = \frac{1}{n} \sum_{i=1}^{n} (t_i - z_i)^2$$

❷ Total number of training examples.

❺ The "**t**" is the target output and the "**z**" is the actual output of an output node. The "**i**" refers to a unique value.

❸ This "**i**" is called the "index of summation." The numbers "**1**" and "**n**" are the lower and upper limits of the summation. "**n**" is equal to the number of training examples.

2. Squared Error (SE)

The Squared Error function is identical to the MSE except it is multiplied by ½, not 1/n.

$$SE = \frac{1}{2} \sum_{i=1}^{n} (t_i - z_i)^2$$

3.Root Mean Square (RMS)

The Root Mean Square performs the same calculations as the MSE, with the only difference being that it squares the answer.

The RMS equation is as follows. *Note: Elements are not labelled because they are the exact same as in the MSE equation.*

$$RMS = \sqrt{\frac{1}{n} \sum_{i=1}^{n} (t_i - z_i)^2}$$

4.The Sum of Square Errors (SSE)

The SSE function is also similar to the MSE, with the only difference being that the answer is not averaged by *n* number of training examples. *Note: Elements are not labelled because they are the exact same as in the MSE equation.*

$$SSE = \sum_{i=1}^{n} (t_i - z_i)^2$$

Why is a Cost Function Used ?

In order for a neural network to successfully train it must minimize the difference between its *actual output* and *target output* to find the *global minimum* (or a local minimum that is close enough to the global). This difference is the *total error*, which essentially tells us how wrong a network is. A cost function provides the *total error* - or difference - between the *target output* and *actual output*.

A Step-by-Step Breakdown: Mean Squared Error (MSE)

Calculating the total error using the Mean Squared Error (MSE) is accomplished by following 4 steps. Demonstrating the MSE will give you an idea of how the SE, RMS and SSE are also calculated.

1. Calculate the *local error* of each output node

$$(t_i - z_i)^2$$

In order to find the *total error*, the *local error* of each training example must first be calculated. Technically, the local error is the difference between a single training example's *actual output* and *target output*.

However....if there are multiple output layer nodes, this means there are multiple actual and target outputs. Hence, the local error is calculated for each node and the results are summed to create the *final local error* for a single training example. If there is only a single output node summing is not required.

Yes, this is somewhat confusing! To help clarify we have included a simple example below.

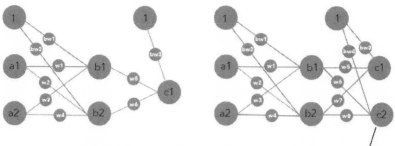

| Single Node Output | Multiple Node Outputs |

1 In this example there are multiple outputs. Therefore, the local error of each output is calculated, and the results are summed to create a final local error.

In the image above, the network on the left has a single output node, and therefore only a single local error to calculate. Once calculated, this single local error becomes the *final local error* of the training example. The image below is an excellent example of how a single *local error* is calculated.

1 The actual output minus the target output.

$$(5\text{-}1)^2$$

However, the network on the right has multiple outputs. Therefore, there are two *local errors* to calculate. Once calculated, these local errors are summed to become the *final local error* of the training example. See below as an example:

$$(5\text{-}1)^2$$ **1**   The local error of **node c1**.

$$(3\text{-}2)^2$$ **2**   The local error of **node c2**.

2. Square each *local error*

$$\left(t_i - z_i\right)^2$$

This action is applied to the local error of every training example (as you can see in the above calculations). Squaring has multiple effects and its benefits are contested! We will cover two effects, the first of which is a fact, and the second which is a contested benefit.

First, the act of squaring means that the difference calculated in Step 1 is treated the same whether it is positive or negative (any number squared, even negative, automatically becomes positive). This is important because it helps the network find a *global minimum* (or a local minimum that is close enough to the global) and also keeps different signs from cancelling each other out, which can lead to a misrepresentation of how wrong the network is.

Second, squaring also helps the network converge faster. Larger derivatives are emphasised for large errors, which helps the network converge faster by taking large steps toward the global minimum. In contrast, smaller derivatives are emphasized for small errors, which helps the network converge faster by taking smaller steps towards the global minimum.

3. Sum the local errors of all training examples

$$\sum_{i=1}^{n}$$

In this step all of the *final local errors* of every training example are summed. If there is only a single training example (as in our mini scenario above) there is no need to sum. Be aware: the **n** in this equation represents training examples, *not individual nodes as in forward propagation*.

4. Multiply and Average!

$$\frac{1}{n}$$

In this final step, 1 is divided by the total number of training examples, **n.** The result is then multiplied against the sum of all local errors (Step 3). This normalizes the sum, which transforms the error into a common frame of reference that we can understand and work with.

Again, if there is only a single training example (as in our mini scenario), there is no need to divide and multiply, since the answer will be 1.

The result of steps 1-4 is the mean squared error, or *total error*. That's it!

Part 3: Fitting it All Together: Review
In this stage we learned about the *cost function*, also commonly called the *loss function*. The cost function calculates the *total error* of a network, which is the difference between the network's actual output and target output. The goal of training a network is to reduce this error to an acceptable level, close to the *global minimum*.

Big Picture
Building on the mathematical functions introduced in Stage 1, the following is a high-level view of everything we have learned so far. To keep things simple, we will begin at node **b2,** which is where we left off in Stage 1: Fitting it All Together.

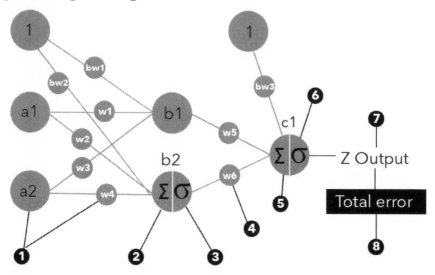

This means we are starting in-between Steps 3 and 4 (as highlighted below).

Step 3-4: The output of **b2** is multiplied by weight **w6**.
Step 5: The result is summed with all other inputs to create the net input of node c, **netc**.
Step 6: **Netc** becomes the input of an activation function.
Step 7: The activation function's output is the *final output of the network*.
Step 8: A cost function is applied to the *output of the network*, and a *total error* is calculated.

Stage 3: Calculate The Gradients

In the last chapter we calculated the *total error* of the network. Now, we are going to discover how this error is spread across every weight in the network so that we can adjust the weights to minimize the error. To do this, we are going to calculate the error of every weight in the network.

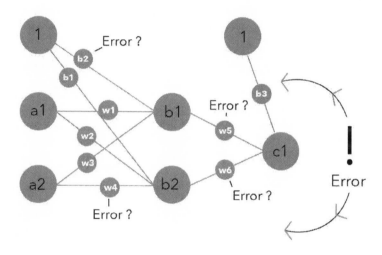

The error of a weight is technically its analytical gradient, and we will use the chain rule to calculate this. Once calculated, the network will work hard to minimize these errors and thus minimize the *total error*. This stage marks the beginning of what is technically called *backpropagation*, also referred to as a *backward pass* or simply *backprop*.

This stage is organized into four sections:

1. Understanding The Mathematical Functions Used
2. Understanding Why Gradients Are Important
3. Learning How To Calculate Gradients
4. Fitting It All Together: Review

Ch. 9
Understanding the Mathematical Functions Used

There are a total of two mathematical functions used in this stage. These functions are used together to calculate the gradient of every weight in a neural network.

- Partial derivative
- Chain Rule

What is a Partial Derivative ?

A partial derivative is best defined by beginning with the definition of a derivative. In mathematics, a derivative represents the rate of change of a function at a single point. Within neural networks this function works with real numbers (any number), which means that the *single point* mentioned above is the slope of the tangent line at a point on a graph.

That is a mouthful, so let's unpack it below with a simple illustration:

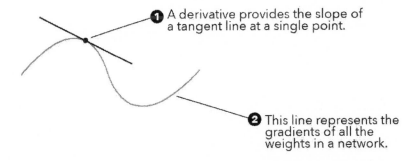

1 A derivative provides the slope of a tangent line at a single point.

2 This line represents the gradients of all the weights in a network.

A partial derivative is the derivative of a function which has two or more variables *but with respect to only one variable*. What's more, all the other variables are treated as constant. In other words, a partial derivative enables you to measure how a single variable (out of many) impacts another single variable. Take for example the black elements in the neural network below.

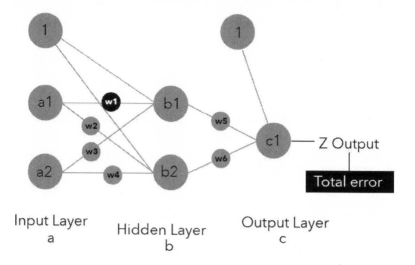

Input Layer
a

Hidden Layer
b

Output Layer
c

The partial derivative allows us to discover how a change in weight **w1** affects the **total error** - while all the other weights remain constant. The same can be calculated for **w2, w3, bw1, bw2 etc.**

The partial derivative is often written using "lower delta y over lower delta x" (meaning the *difference* in y divided by the *difference* in x. To continue with our example above, measuring a change in the **total error** by a change in the weight **w1** would look as follows:

❶ The partial derivative of the **total error**.

$$\frac{\partial E}{\partial W_1}$$

❷ The partial derivative of weight **W1**.

Why is a partial derivative used ?

To update the weights of a neural network we need to know how much a change in a *specific* weight affects the *total error*. That is, we want to find the rate of change between two variables: a specific *weight* and the *total error*. This might seem easy enough, but it poses a problem that can be outlined as follows:

1. There are multiple connected variables (weights, node outputs, node inputs) within a network. *Note: within neural networks variables are often called parameters. Parameter is the correct technical term to use, but we have chosen to use variable for its simplicity.*

2. A slight change in a single weight will affect all variables that occur after it within the network. The larger the network, the greater the impact of a change.
3. Given the ramification of a slight change, calculating how a *specific weight* impacts the *total error* is challenging.
4. Partial derivatives are the answer to this challenge. They enable us to calculate how a function (*total error*) changes with respect to a *single* variable (*specific weight*) while keeping all other variables constant.

One last and important point: within neural networks, the partial derivative is often described as a *gradient*. This is because they are the same! We will touch on this more in Part 2.

What is the chain rule ?

The chain rule is used to find a partial derivative when an equation consists of a function *inside* another function. In other words, it is used to differentiate the function of another function. We will explain this more in depth further on when calculating partial derivatives. For now, here is what the chain rule looks like:

$$\frac{\partial z}{\partial x} = \frac{\partial z}{\partial y} \cdot \frac{\partial y}{\partial x}$$

Why is the chain rule used ?

The best way to answer this is to work from a high-level downwards.

Discovering the error of a specific weight is an important aspect of training a network. In order to discover a weight's error, its partial derivative is calculated. In order to calculate the partial derivative, the chain rule is used multiple times. And that - in a nutshell - is why the chain rule is used.

Ch. 10
Understanding Why Gradient Are Important

Gradients are extremely important and in many ways form the backbone of how a neural network is trained. Let's discover why this is.

What is a gradient?
Within the context of a neural network, a gradient is the following:

- A gradient is the slope of the *local error* for a specific weight. In other words, it is the individual error of a specific weight and it tells us how much a change in a specific weight affects the *total error*.

- A gradient is derived by calculating the partial derivative of a specific weight. In other words, a gradient is a partial derivative. This is very important to understand and cannot be overstated!

When graphed, this is what a gradient looks like. Look familiar ?

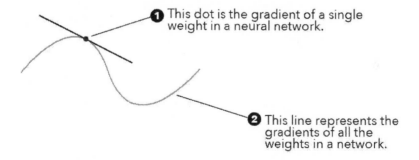

❶ This dot is the gradient of a single weight in a neural network.

❷ This line represents the gradients of all the weights in a network.

Alright. That's fantastic. Let's pull back the curtain even more to get a better understanding.

Gradient importance: in-depth explanation
The goal of this stage is to calculate the gradients for each weight, but why is this important? Let's step back for a minute to answer this question. Training a network involves minimizing the difference between *actual output* and *target output*. This difference is called the *total error* and was

discovered in Stage 2 by using a *cost function.* The question is, once we have discovered the *total error,* what elements can we adjust to minimize it ?

The output of a network is a product of two elements: network input and weights. The input is fixed, so to minimize the *total error* our only option is to adjust the weights. This fact raises a second question that we must answer: how much do we adjust each weight ? Do we increase the weight or decrease the weight?

In other words, what is the exact combination of weights that will produce a minimal *total error* (technically called a *global minimum)* ?

Our answer is *gradient descent,* which is an optimization method that helps us find the exact combination of weights and ultimately discover a *global minimum.*

This, however, raises a third and final question: how do we perform gradient descent?

To perform gradient descent we must calculate the partial derivatives of each weight and then *use the partial derivatives to update each weight.* There are a few ways this can be approached and each has its own pros and cons. Each method, however, has the same goal and begins by calculating partial derivatives. We will explore gradient descent and its various approaches in Stage 5.

Now, back to calculating partial derivatives! When calculating partial derivatives, it is important to realize that there are two different types of weights:

- Weights on the inside of the network situated between input/hidden nodes.
- Weights on the outside of the network situated between a hidden node and output node.

Below is an illustration to help clarify each type:

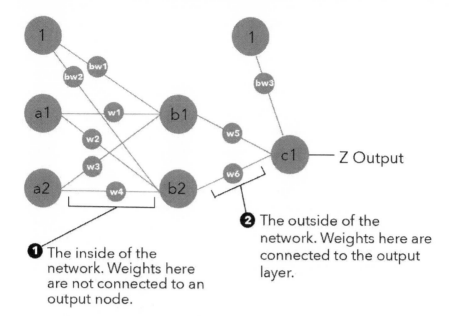

1 The inside of the network. Weights here are not connected to an output node.

2 The outside of the network. Weights here are connected to the output layer.

Now, why is this important? The fact is, each type of weight requires a slightly different method for calculating the partial derivative. What's more, the partial derivatives for output layer weights are *always* calculated *first* because their values are used to calculate the interior partial derivatives.

Let's move on and start calculating the gradients.

Gradient Calculation

The gradient of a weight is the partial derivative of the respective weight. Calculating the partial derivative of an output layer weight and hidden layer weight consists of a number of steps, and each is somewhat different. The same applies to calculating the partial derivatives of bias weights.

This section is organized into the following parts:
1. Calculating The Partial Derivative of Output Layer Weights
2. Calculating The Partial Derivative of Output Layer Bias Weights
3. Calculating The Partial Derivative of Hidden Layer Weights
4. Calculating The Partial Derivative of Hidden Layer Bias Weights

Please remember: the notation you will see is 100% changeable. We have chosen our notation for ease of use and simplicity.

Ch. 11
Calculating the Partial Derivative of Output Layer Weights

This part is divided into the following steps:

Step 1. Discovering The Formula
Step 2. Unpacking The Formula
Step 3. Calculating The Partial Derivatives
Step 4. Compacting The Formula

Step 1/4: Discovering The Formula
The formula below is used to calculate the partial derivative of either a hidden layer or output layer weight. Note what each element stands for.

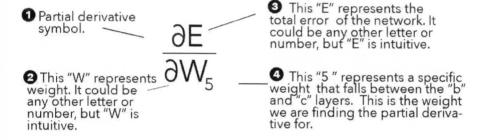

❶ Partial derivative symbol.

❸ This "E" represents the total error of the network. It could be any other letter or number, but "E" is intuitive.

❷ This "W" represents weight. It could be any other letter or number, but "W" is intuitive.

$$\frac{\partial E}{\partial W_5}$$

❹ This "5" represents a specific weight that falls between the "b" and "c" layers. This is the weight we are finding the partial derivative for.

What does this all mean ? Technically the formula is read as: the partial derivative of the *total error* with respect to **w5.** In layman's terms it asks the question: How much does a change in weight **5** affect the *total error* ?

Now, seeing the above is helpful, but what is it *actually* solving for ? The image below helps answer this question with a visual twist. Note the following:

- The elements in **black** are what we are concerned with. Essentially, we want to know how much a change in weight **5** affects the **total error**.
- Remember from Stage 2: The **total error** is computed by applying a *cost function* to the output **z.**

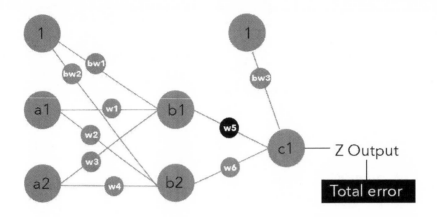

Step 2/4: Unpacking the Formula

The formula above is helpful, but what do we plug into it ? How do we go solve it ? In order to find our answer the formula needs to be unpacked. This is because there are multiple partial derivatives *inside of it,* and to find our answer, we need to unpack all partial derivatives involved.

In other words, **W5** is connected through a series of *partial derivatives* to the **total error**. You can picture this as follows. *Note: the black dots are for multiplication.*

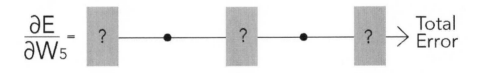

Each of these partial derivatives explains how a certain variable, if changed, affects the variable after it. To put it another way, each partial derivative asks the question: how much does a change in _____ affect _____ ?

To eventually solve our question we need to unpack every single partial derivative, solve each derivative, and multiply the answers together. Our final answer will tell us how a change in weight **w5** affects the **total error.**

The question is, how do we do this? Our answer is the **chain rule**, which helps us quickly unpack partial derivatives. As we apply the chain rule, and for sake of ease, we will label these partial derivatives as *intermediate variables*. This will make it easier for us to distinguish what we are discussing, and is also somewhat intuitive.

First unpacking:

Let's apply the chain rule and unpack our first derivative.

On a high level, working backwards from the **total error,** we can see that there are two *intermediate variables* to be concerned with. First, we need to know how much a change in the output **z** affects the **total error**. Second, we need to know how much a change in weight **w5** affects the output **z**. This constitutes our first unpacking, as you can see below.

❶ The partial derivative of the **total error** with respect to the output **Z**.

$$\frac{\partial E}{\partial W_5} = \frac{\partial E}{\partial Z} \frac{\partial Z}{\partial W_5}$$

❷ The partial derivative of the output **Z** with respect to weight **w5.**

Perfect. As you can see, we have *unpacked* the partial derivative on the left with two partial derivatives on the right. By doing this we have applied the chain rule. However, we can't stop here!

Let's zoom in and unpack the illustration from above.

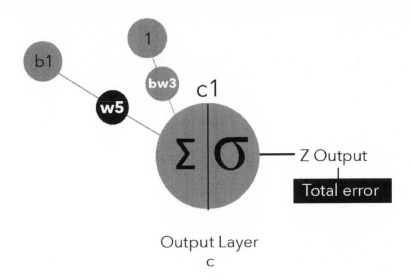

Output Layer
c

As you can see, the output node **c1** is divided into two sections. On the left is the **summation operator** which sums the **net input** into the node. On the right is the **logistic activation function**, which takes the output of the summation operator and applies a function to it before passing it out as the final output **z**.

Second unpacking:

If we pause for a moment, we can see that the partial derivative on the far right of our equation is not fully unpacked. Initially, we thought it went directly from **z** to **w5**, but now we see differently. The fact is, there is still another *intermediate variable* inside of it which tells us how the net input into the node **c1** affects **z** . So, we will apply the **chain rule** to the far right partial derivative and expand it even further.

$$\frac{\partial Z}{\partial W_5} = \frac{\partial Z}{\partial Znet_c} \frac{\partial Znet_c}{\partial W_5}$$

Voila! We are now finished unpacking all of the partial derivatives. Now, once we put everything together our new equation is:

1 The partial derivative of the total error with respect to the output **Z**.

3 The partial derivative of **netc** with respect to weight **w5**.

$$\frac{\partial E}{\partial W_5} = \frac{\partial E}{\partial Z} \frac{\partial Z}{\partial net_c} \frac{\partial net_c}{\partial W_5}$$

2 The partial derivative of **Z** with respect to **netc.**

Finally! Do you see the pattern above ? Our answer is essentially a chain of partial derivatives multiplied together. *Note that the denominator always becomes the numerator for the next partial derivative! This is what links the above together and creates a chain, or a zipper-like structure.*

Step 3/4: Calculating The Partial Derivatives

Our next step is to calculate the partial derivatives, and this is where your calculus needs to shine! We will not be going into great depth for each, but simply summarizing how it is discovered. Working from the left of the equation to the right:

Derivative 1:

$$\frac{\partial E}{\partial Z}$$

This partial derivative is asking the question *how much does a change in z affect the* **total error** *?* To answer this we need to look at the cost function formula, which occurs in between **z** and **total error.** To minimize distraction, here is the cost function formula stripped down with no explanations.

$$MSE = \frac{1}{n} \sum_{i=1}^{n} (t_i - z_i)^2$$

By looking at the *cost function* formula, we can see that the partial derivative is **the negative of the target output - actual output.** Therefore:

① This "**t**" represents the target output of a particular node.

$$\frac{\partial E}{\partial Z} = -(t - z)$$

② This "**z**" represents the actual output of a particular node.

However, for sake of clarity the negatives are often cancelled out.

$$\frac{\partial E}{\partial Z} = (z - t)$$

Derivative 2:

$$\frac{\partial Z}{\partial net_c}$$

This partial derivative is asking the question *how much does a change in* **netc** *affect z?* To answer this we need to look at the *activation function* formula, which occurs in-between **netc** and **z**. Here is the logistic *activation function* formula stripped down with no explanations.

$$f(x) = \frac{1}{1 + e^{-x}}$$

Without going into detail, the answer is found below. It is the derivative of the activation function:

$$\frac{\partial Z}{\partial net_c} = z(1 - z)$$

① Each "**z**" represents the actual output of a particular node.

Derivative 3:

$$\frac{\partial net_c}{\partial W_5}$$

This partial derivative is asking the question *how much does a change in **w5** affect **netc**?*

By looking at the zoomed in illustration, we can see that **netc** is equal to the output of **b1** multiplied by **w5**. This tells us that the answer is the output of **b1**. For sake of clarity we will label the output of b1 as **outb1.**

$$\frac{\partial net_c}{\partial W_5} = out_{b1}$$

Finally! Now that we have calculated all the derivatives we have our full equation. This equation is used to find the partial derivative of any output layer weight. Note the following:

- (**z - t**) and **z(1-t)** remain the same for any output layer weight you are calculating for.
- The variables **w5** and **outb1** will change depending on the weight you are calculating for.

① Derivative 1   **③** Derivative 3

$$\frac{\partial E}{\partial W_5} = (z\text{-}t)\, z(1 - z)\, out_{b1}$$

② Derivative 2

Step 4: Compacting The Formula

Many view the above equation as somewhat clunky and not optimal. In light of this, you will often see the formula compacted even further.

$$\frac{\partial E}{\partial W_5} = \delta_z \text{outb1}$$

❶ This δ_z is the node delta for the output layer. See below for further explanation.

❷ This represents the output of the node **b1**.

What is Delta$_z$? Delta$_z$ is the *node delta*, and it is a term that conveniently sums up 99% of the terms in the full equation. Technically, it is the derivative of **c1's** activation function multiplied by the difference between the *actual output* and *target output*. Here it is unpacked:

$$\delta_z = (z\text{-}t)\, z(1 - z)$$

Calculating the Partial Derivative of Output Layer Bias Weights

---

This part is divided into two sections:

1. It is already calculated
2. Beware: Different Delta$_z$'s

It is Already Calculated

The partial derivative of a hidden node bias weight is very easy to calculate! In fact, we have already calculated it above. It is Delta$_z$!

$$\delta_z = (z\text{-}t)\, z(1 - z)$$

Therefore, if we applied this to the **bw3** weight in our example neural network, it would look as follows:

$$\frac{\partial E}{\partial B_{w3}} = (z\text{-}t)\, z(1 - z)$$

With the above, we are asking the question: *how much does a change in* **bw3** *affect the **total error?*** The answer is our **node delta** that we calculated previously in Part 1. Now, you may be wondering, why is there no **outb1** as in the example below ?

$$\frac{\partial E}{\partial W_5} = \delta_z \, \text{out}_{b1}$$

1 This δ_z is the node delta for the output layer. See below for further explanation.

2 This represents the output of the node **b1**.

The fact is, a bias is not connected to a previous layer and therefore does not have an input. Therefore, we are left with the node delta as the partial derivative of any weight in the output layer.

Beware: Different Delta$_z$'s!

The current example we are using only has a single output node; however, if there are multiple output nodes, the Delta$_z$ changes depending on the partial derivative being calculated! If the incorrect Delta$_z$ is used the partial derivative will be wrong.

To demonstrate this we have included a new network layout below with two output nodes. By looking at it, we can see that **bw3** is connected to **node c1,** while **bw4** is connected to **node c2.**

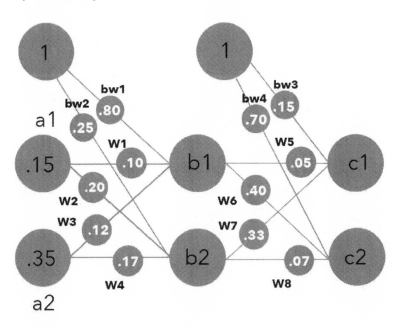

In light of this, **bw3** would make use of the Delta$_z$ for **node c1**, while **bw4** would use the Delta$_z$ for **node c2.**

Ch. 13
Calculating the Partial Derivative of Hidden Layer Weights

Calculating the partial derivative of a hidden layer weight is very similar to that of an output layer weight. In fact, there isn't much difference apart from the level of complexity introduced.

On a high level, we use the same initial formula as above and unpack it using the chain rule.

Let's dig in. This section is divided into the following steps:

Step 1. Discovering the formula
Step 2. Unpacking The Formula
Step 3. Calculating The Partial Derivatives
Step 4. Compacting The Formula

Step 1: Discovering The Formula
The formula below is used to calculate the partial derivative of either a hidden layer node or output layer node. Note the slight difference between this formula and the previous formula for hidden layer weights: in this formula our focus is on **w1**.

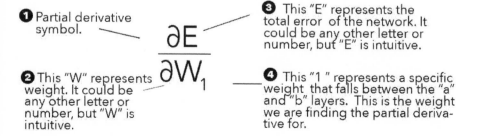

❶ Partial derivative symbol.

❷ This "W" represents weight. It could be any other letter or number, but "W" is intuitive.

$$\frac{\partial E}{\partial W_1}$$

❸ This "E" represents the total error of the network. It could be any other letter or number, but "E" is intuitive.

❹ This "1 " represents a specific weight that falls between the "a" and "b" layers. This is the weight we are finding the partial derivative for.

The question we are trying to solve is: How much does a change in **w1** affect the **total error** ? You can see this visually below.

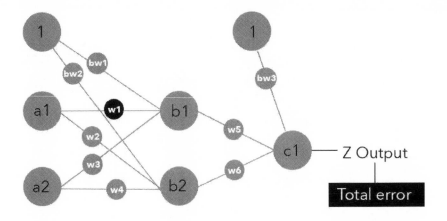

Step 2: Unpacking The Formula

To calculate the partial derivative of **w1** we need to work backwards from the output **Z** to **w1** and compute the partial derivatives of all *intermediate variables*. This is where the complexity of calculating an answer begins to emerge. As you can see above, we are now dealing with a weight that is deeper within the network and therefore affects more variables.

To calculate our answer we must use the chain rule multiple times to unpack lots of partial derivatives - and the more complex a network is, the more difficult this becomes.

As we did before, let's take a closer look at the *edges* we are concerned with to find out exactly what we need to do.

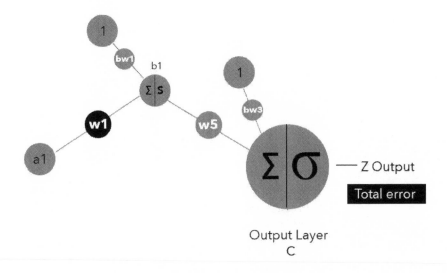

⬆️ First unpacking:

To start let's focus on the area from **a1** to **w5**. When we do this, we can see there are at least two *intermediate variables* to be concerned with. The first is how much a change in the net input of b1 - **netb1** - affects the **total error**. The second is how much a change in weight **w1** affects **netb1**. To clarify, **netb1** is the summation of all inputs into node **b1**. This constitutes our first unpacking, as you can see below.

❶ The partial derivative of the **total error** with respect to **netb1**.

$$\frac{\partial E}{\partial W_1} = \frac{\partial E}{\partial net_{b1}} \frac{\partial net_{b1}}{\partial W_1}$$

❷ The partial derivative of **netb1** with respect to weight **w1**.

⬆️ Second unpacking:

Fantastic. We have now officially used the chain rule and are off to a good start. Our second step is to determine if the partial derivatives we just unpacked can *themselves* be unpacked. Lucky for us, only the first one needs our attention! By looking at the network layout, we can unpack the first partial derivative as follows by applying the chain rule again:

$$\frac{\partial E}{\partial net_{b1}} = \frac{\partial E}{\partial net_{c1}} \frac{\partial net_{c1}}{\partial net_{b1}}$$

Our second unpacking is now complete. However, the partial derivative on the far right *itself* can be unpacked further. Let's use the chain rule one last time.

⬆️ Third unpacking:

$$\frac{\partial net_{c1}}{\partial net_{b1}} = \frac{\partial net_{c1}}{\partial out_{b1}} \frac{\partial out_{b1}}{\partial net_{b1}}$$

We have completed all of our unpacking. Phew! Our formula is now the following. *Note that the numbers above each partial derivative will be used for solving each derivative.*

$$\frac{\partial E}{\partial W_1} = \overset{\textbf{1}}{\frac{\partial E}{\partial net_{c1}}} \overset{\textbf{2}}{\frac{\partial net_{c1}}{\partial out_{b1}}} \overset{\textbf{3}}{\frac{\partial out_{b1}}{\partial net_{b1}}} \overset{\textbf{4}}{\frac{\partial net_{b1}}{\partial W_1}}$$

Step 3: Solving The Derivatives

Our next step is to solve each derivative. We will solve each of the partial derivatives above working from left to right. To help us do this we'll paste in the network image once again. No need to skip back a few pages!

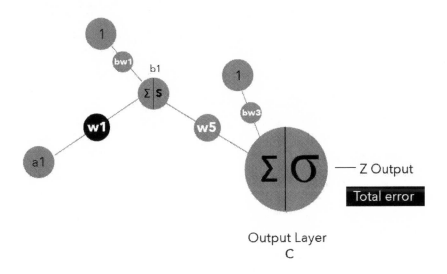

Output Layer
C

Derivative #1

$$\frac{\partial E}{\partial net_{c1}}$$

This partial derivative is asking the question: *how much does a change in* **netc1** *affect the* **total error**? We have already computed this derivative when we calculated the partial derivative of an output layer weight. When we calculated this before, we labelled it as Delta$_z$.

$$\frac{\partial E}{\partial net_{c1}} = \delta_z$$

$$\delta_z = (z\text{-}t)\, z(1 - z)$$

However, before this derivative is solved we must clarify an important point: by changing **netc1**, we impact the net input of *all output nodes* in layer **c**. To reiterate with slightly different language, if we adjust the input to **b1** we impact the input of all nodes in layer **c**.

In light of this, our final partial derivative includes the summation operator. Although the example we are using to demonstrate derivative calculations only contains a single output node, neural networks often contain multiple output nodes.

Therefore, when working with multiple output nodes, the Delta$_z$ for each output node is calculated and all results are summed together.

$$\sum_{c_i} \frac{\partial E}{\partial net_{c_i}}$$

❶ The sum of all net inputs into layer **c** nodes.

For example, if our network example contained two output nodes, the following would be summed together. *Note: the inclusion of w_1 and w_2 will be explained when calculating derivative # 2 below.*

$$\sum_{C} \begin{array}{l} \delta_{z1} = (z\text{-}t)\ z(1-z)\ w_1 \\[6pt] \delta_{z2} = (z\text{-}t)\ z(1-z)\ w_2 \end{array}$$

Combining everything we have done, and for the sake of clarity, we will now label this as the following. *Note that this contains the answer to our partial derivative.*

$$\sum_{C} \delta_z$$

Derivative #2

$$\frac{\partial net_{c1}}{\partial out_{b1}}$$

This partial derivative is asking the question: *how much does a change in* **outb1** *affect* **netc1**? By looking at the network layout, and recalling that the derivative of a constant times the variable is the constant, we can see that the answer is **w5.**

$$\frac{\partial net_{c1}}{\partial out_{b1}} = W_5$$

Here is an important fact: if a network has multiple output nodes, this partial derivative (**w5** in this case) would be multiplied by each Delta$_z$. For example, if a network has two output nodes and two hidden nodes, the following would be calculated. *Note: W_1 and W_2 represent output* *layer weights that are affected by the change made to a single weight in the hidden layer.*

$$\sum_{C} \begin{array}{l} \delta_{z1} = (z\text{-}t)\, z(1-z)\, w_1 \\[1em] \delta_{z2} = (z\text{-}t)\, z(1-z)\, w_2 \end{array}$$

Derivative #3

$$\frac{\partial out_{b1}}{\partial net_{b1}}$$

This partial derivative is asking the question: *how much does a change in* **netb1** *affect* **outb1***?* To answer this we need to look at the *activation function* formula, which occurs in between **netb1** and **outb1.** Here is the *logistic activation function* formula stripped down with no explanations.

$$f(x) = \frac{1}{1 + e^{-x}}$$

Without going into detail, the answer is found below. It is essentially the derivative of the activation function:

$$\frac{\partial out_{b1}}{\partial net_{b1}} = out_{b1}(1 - out_{b1})$$

Derivative #4

$$\frac{\partial net_{b1}}{\partial W_1}$$

This partial derivative is asking the question: *how much does a change in w1 affect netb1?*

By looking at the network illustration, we can see that the answer is the output of **a1**. For sake of clarity, we will label this as **outa1.**

$$\frac{\partial net_{b1}}{\partial W_1} = out_{a1}$$

At last! Now that we have calculated all the derivatives, we have our full equation. Let's put the equation together.

❶ Derivative 1   **❸ Derivative 3**

$$\frac{\partial E}{\partial W_1} = \left(\sum_c \delta_z W_5 \right) out_{b1} (1 - out_{b1}) out_{a1}$$

❷ Derivative 2   **❹ Derivative 4**

Step 4: Compacting The Formula

The above formula is often compacted to make it easier to work with.

❶ This δ represents the layered delta for the node b1.

$$\frac{\partial E}{\partial Z} = \delta_b out_{a1}$$

❷ This represents the output of the node a1.

What is Delta$_b$? Delta$_b$ is the *node delta*, which is an expression that conveniently sums up 99% of the terms in the full equation. Technically, it is the difference between the *actual output* and *target output* of all nodes in layer **c**, multiplied by **w5**, multiplied by the derivative of node **b1's** activation function. Here it is unpacked:

$$\delta_b = \left(\sum_c \delta_z W_5 \right) \text{out}_{b1} (1 - \text{out}_{b1})$$

Ch. 14
Calculating the Partial Derivative of Hidden Layer Bias Weights

This part is divided into two sections:
1. It is Already Calculated
2. Beware: Different Delta$_b$'s !

It is Already Calculated

The partial derivative of a hidden layer bias weight is very similar to an output layer weight. And yes - we have already calculated it! It is the previous layer's node delta, Delta$_b$.

$$\delta_b = \left(\sum_c \delta_z W_i \right) out_i (1 - out_i)$$

❶ All of the letter "**i**"'s refer to a unique value. This value depends on the gradient we are calculating.

Therefore, if we were to apply this to our example network for **bw1**, it would look as follows:

$$\frac{\partial E}{\partial B_{w1}} = \left(\sum_c \delta_z W_5 \right) out_{b1} (1 - out_{b1})$$

With the above, we are asking the question: *how much does a change in* **bw1** *affect the **total error**?* The answer is our **node delta** that we calculated above in Part 3. Again, you may be wondering, why is there no **outa1** as in the example below ?

$$\frac{\partial E}{\partial Z} = \delta_b \, out_{a1}$$

❶ This δ represents the layered delta for the node **b1.**

❷ This represents the output of the node **a1.**

Our answer is the same as when we calculated the output layer weight bias - a bias is not connected to a previous layer and therefore does not have an input. Therefore, we are left with the node delta of a previous layer as the partial derivative of any weight in a hidden layer.

Beware: Different Delta_b 's!

$\square_b$ changes depending on the partial derivative you are calculating for! This is true for both hidden layers and output layers.

To demonstrate this, we have included an additional network layout below. By looking at it, we can see that **bw1** is connected to **node b1,** while **bw2** is connected to **node b2.** In light of this, **bw1** would make use of node **b1's** Delta_b. , while **bw2** would make use of **node b2's** Delta_b. *Note: this will be expanded with an example in Part 3.*

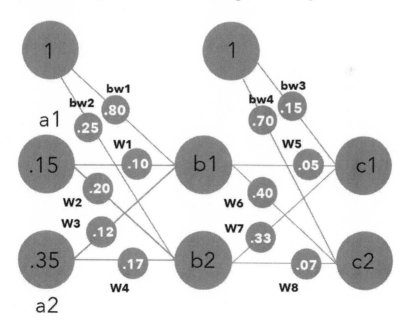

Ch. 15
Fitting it All Together: A Review

This is a very complex stage! However, on a high-level we have learned how to calculate the *gradient* of a weight, which is technically a *partial derivative*. All of the gradients combined create the *total error,* which is computed using a *cost function.*

There are two types of weights: those that are connected to an output node, and those that are not. Calculating the partial derivative for each is a slightly different process. Plus, we learned that the same is true for calculating the partial derivatives of bias weights.

Building on the mathematical functions introduced in Stages 1 and 2, the following is a high-level view of everything we have learned so far. We will begin at the *total error*, which is where we left off in Stage 2: Fitting it All Together. This means we will begin at Step 9, and we will also end there, because it is the only step.

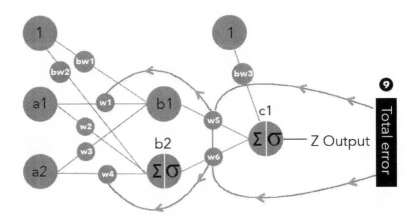

Step 9: As you can see above, the *total error* calculated by the cost function is propagated back through the entire network. What this means is that the *total error* is essentially broken up and distributed back through the network to *every single weight*. The question is, how much of the error should each weight receive ?

This is accomplished by calculating the *partial derivative* for each weight. Remember, the partial derivative asks: How much does a change in a specific weight affect the *total error* ? By calculating the partial derivative of each weight, the network decides how much of the *total error* every weight should receive.

For sake of clarity, in the example above we have removed the former steps (1-8), and placed the *total error* on its side. Please note: the example is very *simple* and not all backpropagation links are shown.

Stage 4: Checking the Gradients

The goal of Stage 4 is to check if the analytical gradient calculations made in Stage 3 are approximately accurate. Many might consider this stage to be optional, and it certainly is; however, gradient checking is very important (especially with deep neural networks), which is why we have opted to include it.

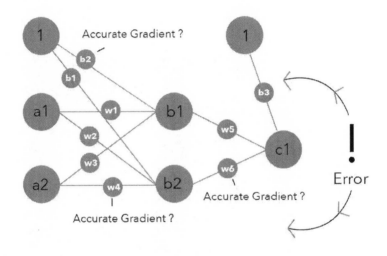

Gradient checking is a very simple procedure that enables the analytical gradients we just calculated to be *manually checked* for accuracy. This is accomplished by using a *numerical estimate* of the partial derivatives - which might sound complex, but it is quite straightforward. Once a gradient has been successfully checked, gradient checking is disabled.

This stage is organized into four sections:

1. Understanding Numerical Estimation
2. Discovering The Formula
3. Calculating The Numerical Estimation
4. Fitting it All Together: Review

Ch. 16
Understanding Numerical Estimation

Deriving all the gradients (partial derivatives) of a neural network is *a lot of* computation, and the more calculations that occur, the greater the probability of an error. Numerical estimation is a fantastic tool that can help minimize these errors. On a high level, numerical estimation essentially checks an analytical gradient against an estimated gradient, and if the value is close to the backpropagation version of the gradient, it passes!

Numerical estimation of the gradient works by creating *two points* to either side of some point on the error curve drawn out by varying a single weight. The slope between those two points is the gradient with respect to that weight, which is shown below:

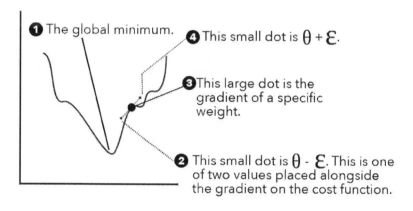

① The global minimum.

④ This small dot is $\theta + \varepsilon$.

③ This large dot is the gradient of a specific weight.

② This small dot is $\theta - \varepsilon$. This is one of two values placed alongside the gradient on the cost function.

In the image above, the gradient of the weight that we are checking is at the large dot, while the small dots on either side of it are the two points we mentioned previously. As you can see, each point consists of a calculation that has two parts: The first is a vector of all the weights in a network, which we call the Greek letter Theta. The second is a small preset number (a hyperparameter), usually denoted by the Greek letter Epsilon.

$$\theta$$
Theta

$$\varepsilon$$
Epsilon

Theta

Theta can be a little tricky to understand because it is actually *two things*:

- It is a vector that contains all of the weights in a network, but...
- It also represents a single, specific weight in a network.

Although Theta is a vector that contains all the weights in a network, in this specific calculation it represents a *single weight* within the network. The weight it represents contains the gradient that we are manually checking, and Epsilon is only added to this weight. If this is confusing, don't worry! It will be expanded on below with an example.

Epsilon

Epsilon is a very small value that is subtracted or added to a weight's gradient to create the *two points* on either side of the gradient. A common value for Epsilon is 10^{-4} (0.0001) or 10^{-5} (0.00001).

Calculating The Numerical Estimate

The numerical estimation is derived by calculating the slope of the two points mentioned above, which can be calculated by using rise over run. Visually, this can be shown as follows:

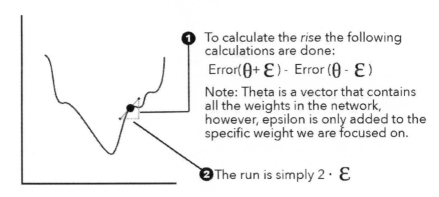

1 To calculate the *rise* the following calculations are done:

$$\text{Error}(\theta + \varepsilon) - \text{Error}(\theta - \varepsilon)$$

Note: Theta is a vector that contains all the weights in the network, however, epsilon is only added to the specific weight we are focused on.

2 The run is simply $2 \cdot \varepsilon$

Discovering the Formula

The formula to calculate the numerical estimate of the gradient of a single weight is below. To tie this back to Section 1, the formula is simply *rise divided by run*.

❶ The Greek letter Theta is a vector that contains all the weights in the network, but don't be mistaken! The Epsilon value is only added to single weight at a time. See below for more details.

$$\frac{Error(\theta + \varepsilon) - Error(\theta - \varepsilon)}{2 \cdot \varepsilon}$$

❷ Epsilon represents a very small number. In this case it is 10^{-4}.

Ch. 18
Calculating the Numerical Estimation

There are 7 steps to calculate and assess the numerical estimate. To help us move through these, we'll break the formula into two parts and calculate them in order.

We'll use an arbitrary weight, **w5,** to illustrate some of the calculations.

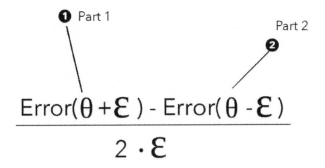

Part 1:

Step 1. Add Epsilon
To start, we add the Epsilon value to the weight we are checking the gradient for. For example, if we are checking the gradient of weight 5, w5, we add epsilon to this to create a new w5 value.

$$W5_{new} = W5 + \varepsilon$$

Step 2. Recalculate The Total Error Of The Network
Next, we recalculate the total error of the network using the value we calculated in Step 1. For example, if we recalculated the value of weight 5, **w5,** we would use this new value instead of the old **w5** value when making our calculations. This means we would work again through Stages 1-2.

This is somewhat challenging to show with an illustration, but on a high level it can be viewed as the following:

$$\text{Error}(\theta + \varepsilon) = \text{Error}(W1, W2, W3, W4, W5 + \varepsilon)$$

Note that the Greek letter Theta is a vector that holds all the weights in a network, but that Epsilon is only added to the weight we are checking the gradient for.

We now have the following part of our formula:

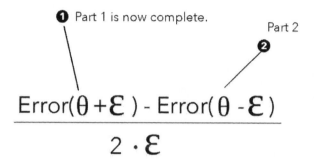

Part 1 is now complete.

Part 2

$$\frac{\text{Error}(\theta + \varepsilon) - \text{Error}(\theta - \varepsilon)}{2 \cdot \varepsilon}$$

Part 2

Step 3. Subtract Epsilon
Moving forward, we recalculate the total error again but this time we subtract the Epsilon value from the weight we are concerned with. Continuing with our example, this means we would subtract Epsilon from **w5.**

$$W5_{\text{new}} = W5 - \varepsilon$$

Step 4. Recalculate The Total Error Of The Network
Finally, we recalculate the total error of the network by using the value we calculated in Step 3. This means we would work again through Stages 1-2.

$$\text{Error}(\theta - \varepsilon) = \text{Error}(W1, W2, W3, W4, W5 - \varepsilon)$$

We have now completed the formula:

❶ Part 1 is now complete.

Part 2 is now complete.

❷

$$\frac{\text{Error}(\theta + \varepsilon) - \text{Error}(\theta - \varepsilon)}{2 \cdot \varepsilon}$$

Step 5: Calculate The Numerical Approximation

Now that we have our entire formula, we can calculate the numerical approximation for the weight we are concerned with. To do this, the formula that we have completed is worked out.

Step 6: Measure Against the Analytic Gradient

Next, we check the numerical approximation against the analytical gradient. Doing this will tell us how "far off" the two gradients are from each other. If you recall, the analytical gradient is the original gradient that the network computed.

Difference = Analytical Gradient - Numerical Gradient

To make the output value easier to work with and interpret, you should convert it to scientific notation. For example:

$$
\begin{aligned}
\textbf{Difference} &= \text{Analytical Gradient - Numerical Gradient} \\
&= 0.000246 - 0.00024599 \\
&= 0.00000001 \\
&= 10^{-8}
\end{aligned}
$$

Step 7: Compute The Relative Error

The output from Step 6 is likely *very small* and thus difficult to interpret. Is it good? Bad? Ok? To help bring clarity, a common practice is to compute the Relative Error and check it against a table of relative errors. The relative error is calculated by dividing the difference by whichever is larger. You can see this below:

$$\text{Relative Error} = \frac{\text{Analytical Gradient - Numerical Gradient}}{\max(\text{Analytical Gradient, Numerical Gradient})}$$

$$= \frac{\text{Difference}}{\max(\text{Analytical Gradient, Numerical Gradient})}$$

The result is converted to scientific notation and then checked against a table of relative error rules of thumb, such as the table below. The goal, of course, is for the numerical gradient to be as close to the analytical gradient as possible, i.e., for the relative error to be as minimal as possible.

Relative Error	Rules of Thumb
$> 10^{-2}$	High chance the gradient is wrong.
$< 10^{-2}$ and $> 10^{-4}$	A double red flag. Something is wrong.
Between 10^{-5} and 10^{-6}	A single red flag. Use caution.
$<= 10^{-7}$	High chance the gradient is correct.

Ch. 19
Fitting it All Together: A Review

In this stage, we covered gradient checking, which is a method that can be used to manually check a computed gradient and make sure it is (more or less) accurate. Gradient checking is optional, but many well-known researchers and scientists within the machine learning field advocate for it.

We learned that gradients are manually checked by creating two fictitious points on either side of a computed gradient, and then calculating the slope of those points - which is rise over run. The result of this is the *numerical estimation* of the gradient, which is then subtracted from the original computed gradient, called the *analytical* gradient.

The end result is the difference between the estimated gradient and the computed gradient, but this difference is often very small, such as 10^{-8}. To make this number more useful, it is often converted to a *relative error* and then checked against a relative error guide, or table.

If the relative error is small enough to be acceptable, the computed gradient is considered valid and passes the test.

Stage 5: Updating the Weights

The goal of Stage 5 is to update the weights in a neural network. This is accomplished by continuing to apply the *backpropagation* we began in Stage 3 *by using* the gradients we calculated in Stage 3 through an optimization process known as *gradient descent*. That's a mouthful - but don't worry, we will unpack it all below.

This stage is organized into four sections:
1. What is Gradient Descent ?
2. Methods of Gradient Descent
3. Updating the Weights
4. Fitting it All Together: Review

Ch. 20
What is Gradient Descent?

Gradient descent is an optimization method that helps us find the exact combination of weights for a network that will minimize the output error. It is how we *turn the dials* on our network and fine tune it so that we are satisfied with its output. A good way to approach gradient descent is simply by unpacking its name. Let's start there!

- *Gradient* essentially means slope.
- *Descent* means to descend, or go down.
- Therefore, *gradient descent* has something to do with descending down a slope.

Perfect. This now raises a few questions:

- What are we descending ?
- What is the slope ?
- How fast do we descend ?

With *gradient descent,* we descend down the slope of gradients to find the *lowest point*, which is where the *error* is smallest. Remember, the gradients are the errors of the individual weights, and the goal of a network is to minimize these errors. By descending down the gradients we are actively trying to minimize the *cost function* and arrive at the *global minimum.*

Our steps are determined by the steepness of the slope (the gradient itself) and the *learning rate.*

The learning rate is a value that speeds up or slows down how quickly an algorithm learns. Technically, it is a hyperparameter set in the pre-stage that determines the size of step an algorithm takes when moving towards a *global minimum.*

Most study cases you will find online make use of learning rates between 0.0001 and 1. You can read more on the learning rate in our extended definitions section.

Back to gradient descent. To give an intuitive explanation of how gradient descent *works* and its *goal*, many textbooks use the analogy of a person hiking down a mountain. It is quite helpful, so we have decided to include it. *Note that the goal is, of course, to reach the bottom where the global minimum lies.*

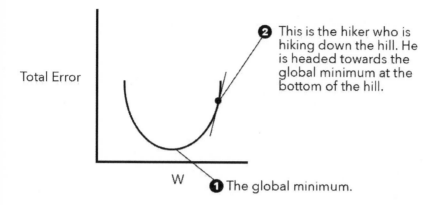

Do you see a potential problem though ? The above is a simple representation that does not take into consideration the complexity of *real-life* neural networks. In practice, neural networks have *hundreds* if not *thousands* of weights which completely change the landscape of the simple graph above.

In fact, what if the terrain the hiker was descending is not smooth, but has many *local minima* that he can become stuck in and falsely believe is the *global minimum* ? See the example below. Again, it is extremely simplified.

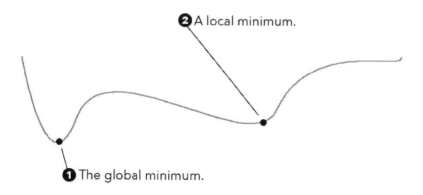

This is a potential pitfall that all neural networks face when using gradient descent. It also reflects the reality of the world we live in and the data we collect as input: it's messy, imperfect, and hard to work with. So, what can we do? To help mitigate the problem an optimization algorithm is typically used in conjunction with back propagation.

A popular example is *Momentum*, which is used to help push the algorithm out of a *local minimum*. It essentially adds a boost to the direction the network is moving in. *Momentum* does not always work, but it is a popular technique often used with the backpropagation algorithm. Alongside the *learning rate, momentum* is preset for the algorithm in Stage 1.

Other optimization methods include the *Nesterov accelerated gradient* (which fine tunes *momentum*), *Adagrad, Adadelta (Adagrad extension), RMSprop, and Adam.*

Ch. 21
Gradient Descent Methods

This section is divided into the following parts:
1. Introduction
2. Batch Gradient Descent
3. Stochastic Gradient Descent (SGD)
4. Mini-Batch Gradient Descent

Introduction

In Stage 3, we calculated all of the partial derivatives for every weight in the network. Now we can update these weights using gradient descent. There are a number of different approaches to implementing gradient descent, and remember: matrix multiplication is used in each to compute the gradients! You can skip back to Stage 3 to review matrix multiplication if necessary.

On a high level, the methods differ with regards to how much data is used before a weight is adjusted. Each method has its own pros and cons as well as advocates, but practically speaking, the significant tradeoffs include time and accuracy.

Here is an interesting fact: networks will often make use of two or more methods to achieve the *global minimum* (although not at the same time; only a single method can be used at one time). For example, a network might begin training using SGD, and then switch to Batch once the noise created by SGD begins to interfere with convergence. There are many strategies and theories on how to select the best method, but those are beyond this introductory text.

Below is a very brief explanation of three gradient descent methods:

Batch Gradient Descent (also called Full-Batch)

Full-Batch training works by summing the gradients for every training set element and then updating the weights. This updating is technically one iteration (also called an epoch). For example, if a training set consists of 10,000 images, by definition it also contains 10,000 elements. With this example, an update of the weights will not occur until after the gradients of all 10,000 images have been calculated and combined.

As you can imagine, this type of training can be very slow. Unlike SGD however (see below), Batch training is guaranteed to find a local minimum on a non-convex surface and *global minimum* on a convex surface. See below for an example of convex vs non-convex.

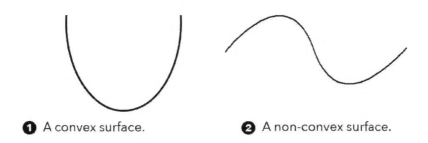

❶ A convex surface.   **❷** A non-convex surface.

Stochastic Gradient Descent (also called SGD / Online)

With SGD, the weights in a network are modified after *every training set element*. What this means is that a *single* training set element is used to update a parameter (weight) in a particular iteration. For example, if a training set consists of 10,000 images, each image is a training set element (and all examples combined to form a training set).

With SGD, it is important to note that the training set is shuffled because the order of the data can cause the network to become biased. There are various approaches to shuffling, such as a single shuffle at the beginning of training or after every epoch.

SGD is typically faster than full-batch training, especially early on in the training process. However, it can also produce much more noise, which causes the network to bounce around near the *global minimum* but never reach it.

Mini-Batch Gradient Descent

Mini-Batch training works by summing the gradients for multiple training set elements (but not all of them) and then updating the weights. The size of the mini-batch can be preset as a hyperparameter or randomly chosen by the algorithm.To continue with our example above, these elements would be n number of images from our training set of 10,000 images.

Mini-Batch falls somewhere in between Full-Batch and SGD, and has been used very successfully with neural networks. It also tends to be one of the most popular gradient descent methods.

Ch. 22
Updating Weights

Updating the weights of a neural network is quite straightforward, at least compared to computing the gradients! *Note that updating bias weights is no different than updating any other weight. The exact same formula is used.*

This section is divided into the following parts:
1. General Weight Update Equation
2. Batch Training Weight Update Equation
3. SGD Training Weight Update Equation
4. Mini-Batch Training Weight Update Equation

General Weight Update Equation
The general equation for updating a weight is given below. Note that the equation is slightly altered depending on the gradient descent method used. These alterations will be explored further on.

Remember, the big idea is to continue applying this update rule so that the algorithm can *descend* the gradients and minimize the cost function. The weight update formula does this by taking a step in the *opposite direction* of a weight's gradient. See below.

Note: For the equations below we have continued using the notation from previous examples.

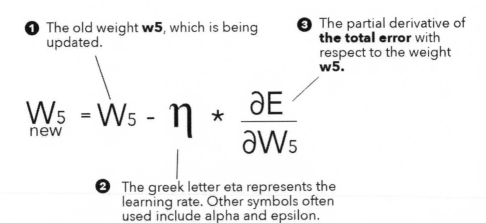

❶ The old weight **w5**, which is being updated.

❸ The partial derivative of **the total error** with respect to the weight **w5.**

$$W_{5\,new} = W_5 - \eta * \frac{\partial E}{\partial W_5}$$

❷ The greek letter eta represents the learning rate. Other symbols often used include alpha and epsilon.

New weight = old weight - learning rate x the partial derivative of the *total error* with respect to weight **w5** .

Working from right to left, what we are doing is multiplying the error (which is the partial derivative) by the learning rate and subtracting that from the current weight we are focused on. As a result, we are basically cancelling out that weight's contribution to the error.

Big Picture Reading
The whole idea behind gradient descent is to minimize the error of every single weight in a neural network, which results in the *total error* of the network being minimized. In the equation above, the **subtraction** operation is what enables this to happen!

The error of the current weight is *subtracted from the current weight* **w5**. This is what enables the network to take a step *down the slope* and minimize the weight's error. To help speed this up or slow it down, it is multiplied by a *learning rate*.

Batch Training Weight Update Equation
For batch training, the weights are updated after passing an entire training set through the network; that is, after one epoch has been completed. The following equation is used:

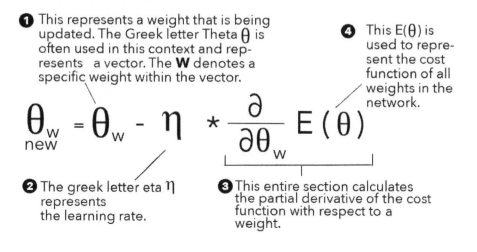

1 This represents a weight that is being updated. The Greek letter Theta θ is often used in this context and represents a vector. The **W** denotes a specific weight within the vector.

4 This $E(\theta)$ is used to represent the cost function of all weights in the network.

$$\theta_{w_{new}} = \theta_w - \eta * \frac{\partial}{\partial \theta_w} E(\theta)$$

2 The greek letter eta η represents the learning rate.

3 This entire section calculates the partial derivative of the cost function with respect to a weight.

Technical Reading: Left to Right
New weight = old weight - learning rate multiplied by the partial derivative of the *total error* with respect to a weight, **w.**

Working from right to left, what we are doing is multiplying the error (which is the partial derivative) of a weight by the learning rate and subtracting that from the current weight we are focused on.

Big Picture Reading
The purpose of a weight update is to minimize the error of a weight and help move the network towards minimizing the *total error*.

Now, this formula makes use of the Greek letter **Theta** and letter **w.**
Theta is a vector that contains all of the weights in the network, while **w** is used to denote a specific weight *within* the vector.
Theta can be pictured as a line that contains all the weights in a network:

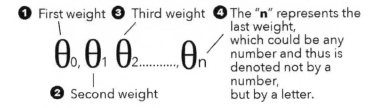

❶ First weight ❸ Third weight ❹ The "n" represents the last weight, which could be any number and thus is denoted not by a number, but by a letter.

$$\theta_0, \theta_1, \theta_2 \ldots \ldots, \theta_n$$

❷ Second weight

To understand this further, let's unpack the far right side of the batch training equation. In the equation above this is labelled as **#3.**

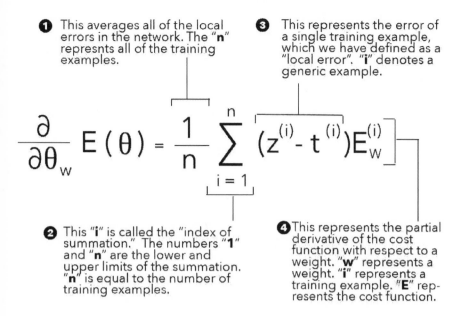

① This averages all of the local errors in the network. The "**n**" represnts all of the training examples.

③ This represents the error of a single training example, which we have defined as a "local error". "**i**" denotes a generic example.

$$\frac{\partial}{\partial \theta_w} E(\theta) = \frac{1}{n} \sum_{i=1}^{n} (z^{(i)} - t^{(i)}) E_w^{(i)}$$

② This "**i**" is called the "index of summation." The numbers "**1**" and "**n**" are the lower and upper limits of the summation. "**n**" is equal to the number of training examples.

④ This represents the partial derivative of the cost function with respect to a weight. "**w**" represents a weight. "**i**" represents a training example. "**E**" represents the cost function.

As you can see above, batch training makes use of the average sum of all the training example errors in a network. Note: **z - t** is the *actual output - target output.*

SGD Training Weight Update Equation

For SGD training, the weights are updated after each training set element is passed through the network. This approach uses the same equation as the general equation given at the top of this section. Here is the equation again:

① The old weight **w5**, which is being updated.

③ The partial derivative of **the total error** with respect to the weight **w5.**

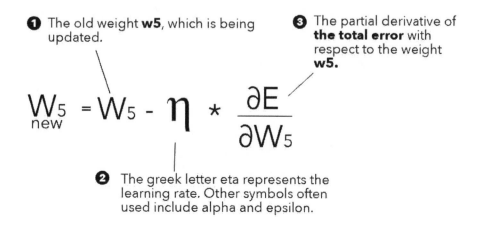

$$W_{5_{new}} = W_5 - \eta * \frac{\partial E}{\partial W_5}$$

② The greek letter eta represents the learning rate. Other symbols often used include alpha and epsilon.

Technical Reading: Left to Right
New weight = old weight - learning rate multiplied by the partial derivative of the *total error* with respect to a weight, **w.**

Working from right to left, what we are doing is multiplying the error (which is the partial derivative) of a weight by the learning rate and subtracting that from the current weight we are focused on.

Big Picture Reading
With SGD, weights are updated after each single training example is passed through the network. This is why the equation above does not use the summation operator as in batch training.

Mini-Batch Training Weight Update Equation
For mini-batch training the weights are updated after a certain number of training elements have passed through the network. In the equation below, the batch size is set to 10 training examples.

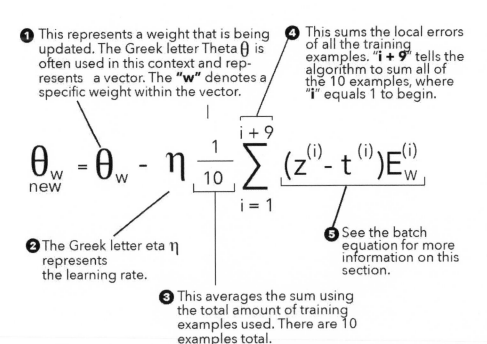

1 This represents a weight that is being updated. The Greek letter Theta θ is often used in this context and represents a vector. The **"w"** denotes a specific weight within the vector.

4 This sums the local errors of all the training examples. "**i + 9**" tells the algorithm to sum all of the 10 examples, where "**i**" equals 1 to begin.

$$\theta_{w}^{new} = \theta_{w} - \eta \frac{1}{10} \sum_{i=1}^{i+9} (z^{(i)} - t^{(i)}) E_{w}^{(i)}$$

2 The Greek letter eta η represents the learning rate.

5 See the batch equation for more information on this section.

3 This averages the sum using the total amount of training examples used. There are 10 examples total.

The equation can be read as follows from left to right: New weight = old weight - learning rate multiplied by the averaged sum of the partial derivatives of all training examples.

In this case there are a total of 10 training examples in the mini-batch. Hypothetically, if there were 1000 training examples in the training set, updates would occur every 10 training examples. Thus, there would be a total of 100 weight updates.

Ch. 23
Fitting it All Together: A Review

At this stage, we have learned how the weights in a neural network are updated. At a high level, this is accomplished by moving in the opposite direction of each gradient (partial derivative), calculated in Stage 3. This process is called *gradient descent* due to the fact that the goal is to move *down* the gradients to find the lowest error.

We also learned that there are three popular methods for applying gradient descent, including Batch gradient descent, Stochastic gradient descent, and Mini-batch gradient descent. Each varies in the amount of data used to update and the time it takes to update.

Constructing a Network: Hands-On Example

In this chapter we will build a simple neural network using all the concepts and functions we learned in the previous few chapters. Our example will be basic but hopefully very intuitive. Many examples available online are either hopelessly abstract or make use of the same data sets, which can be repetitive.

Our goal is to be crystal clear and engaging, but with a touch of fun and uniqueness.

This chapter is divided into the following sections:

1. Defining the Scenario
2. Pre-Stage: Network Structure
3. Stage 1: Running Data Through the Network
4. Stage 2: Calculating the Total Error
5. Stage 3: Calculating the Gradients
6. Stage 4: Gradient Checking
7. Stage 5: Updating the Weights
8. Wrapping it All Up: Final Review

Defining the Scenario: Man vs Chicken

On a high level we are going to build a neural network that can distinguish between two 8x8 grayscale pixel characters: man or chicken. To do this we will systematically work through each of the stages we learned about in the previous chapters.

8 pixels in width

8 pixels in height

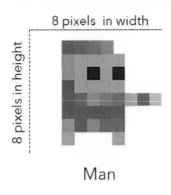

Man

8 pixels in width

8 pixels in height

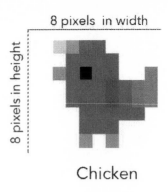

Chicken

Now, if we were to create this entire network and perform all the calculations, this example would be extremely long and repetitive - not to mention a nightmare for display on a Kindle.

With that being said, we are only going to follow one of our characters as it is broken apart and fed through the network - and in a very, VERY simplified manner. This will provide you with a good idea of how each mathematical function operates. Ready to go ? Let's dig in.

Note: Convolutional neural networks (CNN's) - and not traditional feedforward networks - are typically used for image classification. CNN's performance is superior in this regard, which is why major technology companies such as Google and Facebook use CNN's to classify images. However, images provide a fantastic visual that can help in the teaching process, which is precisely why we will be using them!

Pre-Stage: Network Structure

This stage is organized into the following sections:
1. Determining Structural Elements
2. Understanding the Input Layer
3. Understanding the Output Layer
4. Simplifying our Network
5. Stage Review

Section 1: Determining Structural Elements
In this stage we need to define a number of structural elements.

Total input nodes: 64.
This number is derived from each image, which is 8x8 pixels.

Total hidden layers: 1.
We will follow Stanford's Andrew Ng's recommendation, which is to begin with a single hidden layer.

Total hidden nodes: 64.
Again, we will follow popular opinion and use the same number of hidden nodes as input nodes. It is a good place to start.

Total output nodes: 2.
Due to the fact that we are classifying two elements we will use two output nodes. Each node will represent a unique class: man or chicken. If we pass an image of a chicken through the network, our goal is for the output node that represents the *chicken* class to output a **"1"**, and the man class output a **0 (zero)**.

Likewise, if we pass an image of a man through the network, our goal is for the output node that represents the *man* class to output a **"1"**, and the chicken class output a **0 (zero)**.

Bias value: 1.
We will set our bias' to have a value of 1. Again, this is common practice.

Weight values: Random
We will assign random values to begin.

Learning rate: 0.5
We will begin with an initial learning rate of 0.5. This number is somewhat arbitrary, and it can be changed as the network learns.

Now that we have selected all of our structural elements, let's take a look at our neural network architecture. Note that due to its size, not all nodes and weights can be shown. There are over 4200 weights in total - plus 132 nodes (including biases). In light of this, we will be working with a simplified version of our network.

However, on a grand scale our network appears as follows:

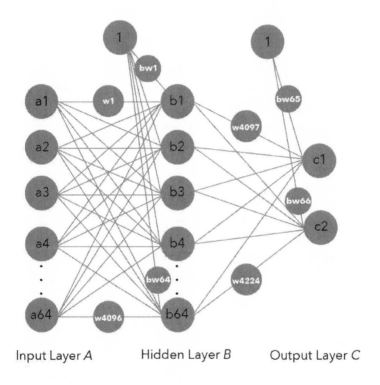

Input Layer *A*   Hidden Layer *B*   Output Layer *C*

Before we transition to a simplified version of our network it is a good idea to take a closer look at the input and output layers.

Section 2: Understanding the Input Layer
Our input layer has a total of 64 input nodes. As you can see in the chicken image below, this is because each pixel becomes a node in the input layer.

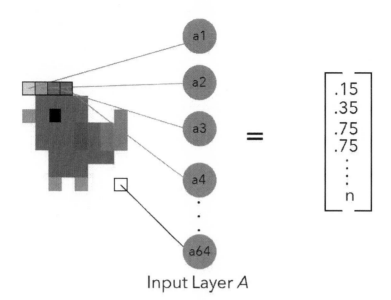

Input Layer *A*

If you remember, all input features are stored within a vector, which is also shown on the far right of the image. But what about the numbers inside the vector ? Where are they coming from? Let's zoom in once more to find our answer.

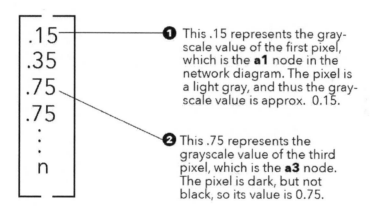

1 This .15 represents the gray-scale value of the first pixel, which is the **a1** node in the network diagram. The pixel is a light gray, and thus the gray-scale value is approx. 0.15.

2 This .75 represents the grayscale value of the third pixel, which is the **a3** node. The pixel is dark, but not black, so its value is 0.75.

As you can see above, the numbers in the vector represent the grayscale value of each node in the input layer. The *n* represents the grayscale value of the last input node, node 64.

Section 3: Understanding the Output Layer

The output layer has two nodes, and as we mentioned in the pre-stage, each node represents a specific class: man or chicken.

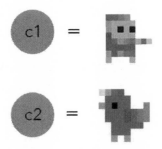

Each training image we put through the network has a target output assigned to it which is stored in a vector. In the example below, if we put an image of a chicken through the network, our target output is a vector containing 0 (zero) on the top and 1 below. The reverse is also true for an image of a man. This is technically called *one-hot encoding*.

One-hot encoding is method that transforms categorical features (such as our man and chicken) into a new format of 1's and 0 (zeros). This format is popular because it has proven to work very well with classification and regression algorithms.

With one-hot encoding, the correct target output node is "hot", i.e., 1, while the rest are 0 (zero).This is why when we pass a chicken through, we want the output to be a vector as close to the following as possible:

*Note that **0 (zero)** is the output of **node c_1**, and **1** is the output of **node c_2**.*

Section 4: Simplifying our Network

To finish off this stage, let's take a look at the simplified version of this network we will be working with. This will require a mental leap and some imagination! What we will be doing is reducing our entire image classifying network to a handful of nodes, which makes it much easier to work with as an example, especially on a Kindle.

Specifically, we will imagine that our image can be classified using only two input nodes and two hidden nodes. To do this we will continue using the input values we introduced earlier for **a1** and **a2**. These inputs have values of 0.15 and 0.35, which should make for an interesting case study.

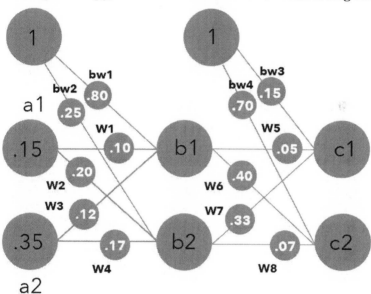

Section 5: Stage Review

In this stage we created our network structure, which includes the number of input nodes, hidden nodes/layers, output nodes, bias values, weight values, and the learning rate. We also concluded the following:

- If the input is a man, we want the output to be a vector of [1, 0].
- If the input is a chicken, we want the output to be [0, 1].

We also learned about how an image is broken down, pixel, by pixel, and stored within an input vector. Lastly, we simplified the structure so that it can be used for teaching purposes.

Let's move on to Stage 1 and begin to move our input through the network.

Stage 1: Running Data Through the Network

It's now time to run our input data through the network. If applicable, answers will be rounded to a maximum of four decimal places.

This stage is divided into three sections:
1. Moving From the Input Layer to the Hidden Layer
2. Moving From the Hidden Layer to the Output Layer
3. Stage Review

Section 1: Moving From the Input Layer to the Hidden Layer

Let's begin by calculating the net input to nodes **b1 and b2,** which we will label as **netb1 and netb2,** respectively.

To calculate **netb1 and netb2**, we need to sum all of the inputs into nodes **b1** and **b2**. Using the **summation operator**, here is what this would look like for **netb1.**

❶ **"n"** stands for total number of nodes that must be multiplied by their respective weights.

$$netb1 = \sum_{i=1}^{n} (a_i \, w_i) + bias$$

❷ "**a**" and "**w**" stand for the output of a node and its respective weight. The "**i**" indicates a unique value.

As we learned in Part 2: Stage 2, the above can be written as follows:

netb1 = (outa1 * w1) + (outa2 * w3) + (bias * bw1)

And when we substitute with our values, we find our answer:

netb1 = (0.15 * 0.10) + (0.35 * 0.12) + (1 * 0.80) **= 0.857**

The exact same is done for **netb2.**

netb2 = (outa1 * w2) + (outa2 * w4) + (bias * bw2)

And substitution yields our answer:

netb2 = (0.15 * 0.20) + (0.35 * 0.17) + (1 * 0.25) = **0.3395**

Let's see how this looks within our network. Remember, each net input value will be put through an activation function before it leaves its respective node.

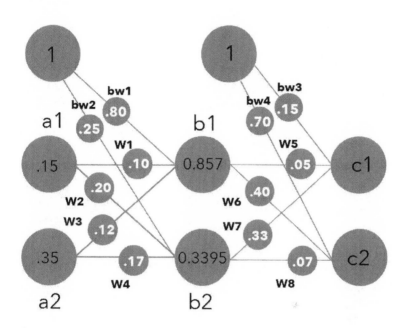

Section 2: Moving From the Hidden Layer to the Output Layer

This section is divided into the following:

1. Introduction
2. Applying B1 and B2 Activation Functions
3. Moving From Layer B to C

Introduction

To move our values from the hidden layer to the output layer, we must first apply an activation function to our net input values. This will provide us with the output for our hidden nodes, which we can then move forward along their respective edges.

Here is a picture of a node to remind you of how the summation operator and activation function work together:

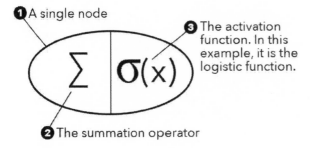

① A single node

③ The activation function. In this example, it is the logistic function.

② The summation operator

Applying B1 and B2 Activation Functions

Here is the Logistic activation function with highlights for **node b1**.

$$f(x) = \frac{1}{1 + e^{-x}}$$

① This **negative x** represents the net input of b1, or **netb1**.

② This **"e"** is a mathematical constant. Its value is approximately 2.71828.

Now, let's substitute our value for **netb1**, along with the constant **e**.

$$f(netb1) = \frac{1}{1 + 2.71828^{-0.857}}$$

$$= \frac{1}{1.424433719}$$

$$= 0.7020$$

Now, let's do the same for **netb2.**

$$f(x) = \frac{1}{1 + e^{-x}}$$

① This **negative x** represents the net input of b2, or **netb2**.

② This **"e"** is a mathematical constant. Its value is approximately 2.71828.

Substituting:

$$f(netb2) = \frac{1}{1 + 2.71828^{-0.3395}}$$

$$= \frac{1}{1.71212646}$$

$$= \quad 0.5841$$

Fantastic! We have now calculated the outputs of nodes **b1** and **b2.** If we update the values of each hidden node, the network now looks as follows:

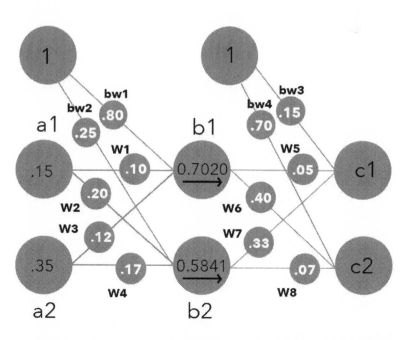

Moving From Layer B to C

All we need to do now is move this output to **nodes c1** and **c2.** To do this, we will follow the same steps as we did previously when me moved from the input layer to the hidden layer. Since we have already explained the steps involved, we will only show the calculations.

To calculate **netc1:**

netc1 = (outb1 * w5) + (outb2 * w7) + (bias * bw3)

We then substitute our values to find our answer:

netc1 = (0.7020 * 0.05) + (0.5841 * .33) + (1 * 0.15) = **0.3779**

To calculate **netc2:**

netc2 = (outb1 * w6) + (outb2 * w8) + (bias * bw4)

Substituting:

netc2 = (0.7020 * 0.40) + (0.5841 * .07) + (1 * 0.70) = **1.0217**

Our last step in this stage is to apply an activation function to **netc1** and **netc2.** This will provide us with the final outputs of the network. We will continue using the Logistic activation function.

$$f(netc1) = \frac{1}{1 + 2.71828^{-0.3779}}$$

$$= \frac{1}{1.685299201}$$

$$= 0.5934$$

And for **netc2:**

$$f(netc2) = \frac{1}{1 + 2.71828^{-1.0217}}$$

$$= \frac{1}{1.359982697}$$

$$= \quad 0.7353$$

The final outputs for the network are **0.5934** and **0.7353**. Let's wrap up this stage with a top-down view:

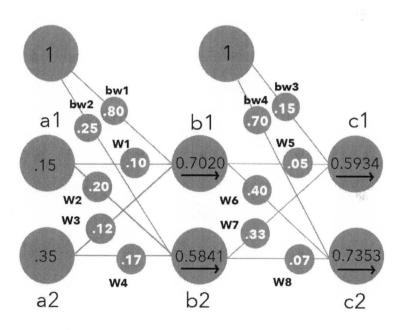

Stage Review:

In this stage we moved our input through the network to create a final output. To do this we made use of two mathematical functions: the summation operator and an activation function. Each of these functions was used twice for each node as we moved the input through the network.

We also made use of **e,** which is a mathematical constant with a value of approximately 2.71828.

Stage 2: Calculating the Total Error

It is now time to calculate the total error of the network! To do this, we will compare the actual output of the network to the target output of the network. If you recall, a target output is provided for each training example that is passed through the network. In our case, our training example is an image of a chicken, and our target output is a vector with a value of 0 (zero) for **node c1** and value of 1 for **node c2.**

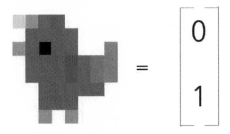

With that being said, let's move forward and calculate the total error of our network. Our total error will be the combined *local error* of each output node. To calculate this, we need to apply a **cost function** to each output node. For this example, we will use the Squared Error (SE) function.

The SE formula is below. Note that we have highlighted elements for output layer c:

❷ This squares the output node(s) error(s), which has multiple effects.

$$SE = \frac{1}{2} \sum_{i=1}^{n} (t_i - z_i)^2$$

❸ The "t" is the target output and the "z" is the actual output of each output node in **layer c**. The "i" refers to a unique value.

❶ This "i" is called the "index of summation." The numbers "1" and "n" are the lower and upper limits of the summation. "n" is equal to the number of training examples.

To find our total error we will apply the cost function to each output node, and then sum the answers together. Since we are only concerned with a single training example there is no need to sum over all training examples, which means we will ignore the summation operator.

Calculating the Local Error of Node c1

To start, we'll substitute our values to find the local error for **node c1**.

$$SE_{c1} = (0 - 0.5934)^2$$
$$= -0.5934^2$$
$$= 0.3521$$

Calculating the Local Error of Node c2

We will follow the same steps for **node c2**.

$$SE_{c2} = (1 - 0.7353)^2$$
$$= 0.2647^2$$
$$= 0.070$$

Finally, we will sum our local errors to discover the final local error.

$$SE = 0.3521 + 0.070$$
$$= 0.4221$$

Now that we have the final local error, we can plug it into our cost function formula.

$$SE = \frac{1}{2} * 0.4221$$
$$= 0.21105$$

There we have it! **Our total error is 0.21105.** Let's see what this looks like from a high-level:

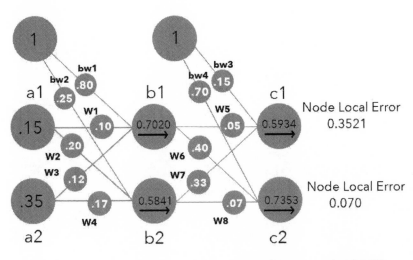

Stage Review:

This stage was quite brief. In this stage we calculated the total error of the network by applying a cost function to the actual output of the network. Since there are two outputs, we applied the cost function to each, summed the results and multiplied by 1/2 to find the total error.

Stage 3: Calculating the Gradients

Since we have successfully moved our inputs through the network and calculated our total error, we can now begin backpropagation!

Due to the above, this stage is divided into the following sections:
1. Calculating Gradients for Output Layer Weights
2. Calculating Output Layer Bias Weights
3. Calculating Gradients for Hidden Layer Weights
4. Calculating Hidden Layer Bias Weights
5. All Gradients

Section 1: Calculating Gradients For Output Layer Weights

We will begin by calculating the partial derivative for **weight w5** using the derivative formula we learned in Part 2: Stage 3. To do this we will work step-by-step through the problem, and then follow the same steps for weight **w6.** For the remaining weights we will summarize the answers. Below is a quick visual to help provide context.

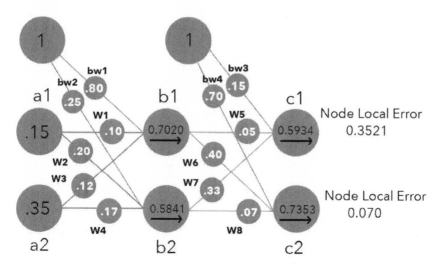

Calculating the gradient with respect to w5

The formula we will use is directly below. To refresh your memory, the formula is essentially asking the question: How much does a change in weight **w5** affect the **total error** ? Note that the "t" and "z" in the equation only apply to **node c1**. This is because **w5** only affects **node c1**. For clarification take a peek back at the network layout above!

1 Every "**z**" in this formula is the actual output for **node c1**.

$$\frac{\partial E}{\partial W_5} = (z-t) \; z(1-z) \; out_{b1}$$

2 This "**t**" is the target output for **node c1**.

Substituting our values, we get the following:

$$\frac{\partial E}{\partial W_5} = (0.5934 - 0) * 0.5934(1-0.5934) * 0.7020$$

$$= 0.5934 * 0.5934(0.4066) * 0.7020$$

$$= 0.1005$$

Calculating the gradient with respect to w6

The formula we will use is below. Note what changes though! The "t" and "z" in this equation only apply to **node c2**. This is because **w6** only affects **node c2**.

1 Every "**z**" in this formula is the actual output for **node c2**.

$$\frac{\partial E}{\partial W_6} = (z-t) \; z(1-z) \; out_{b1}$$

2 This "**t**" is the target output for **node c2**.

Substituting our values:

$$\frac{\partial E}{\partial W_6} = (0.7353 - 1) * 0.7353 (1 - 0.7353) * 0.7020$$

$$= -0.2647 * 0.7353(0.2647) * 0.7020$$

$$= -0.0362$$

Now for a quick calculation of **w7** and **w8.**

Calculating the gradient with respect to w7

Notice that this calculation is almost identical to **w5.** The only difference is replacing **outb1** with **outb2.**

$$\frac{\partial E}{\partial W_7} = (0.5934 - 0) * 0.5934(1 - 0.5934) * 0.5841$$

$$= 0.5934 * 0.5934(0.4066) * 0.5841$$

$$= 0.0836$$

Calculating the gradient with respect to w8

Notice that this calculation is almost identical to **w6.** Again, **outb1** has been replaced with **outb2.**

$$\frac{\partial E}{\partial W_8} = (0.7353 - 1) * 0.7353(1 - 0.7353) * 0.5841$$

$$= -0.2647 * 0.7353(0.247) * 0.5841$$

$$= -0.0301$$

Section 2: Calculating Gradients For Output Layer Bias Weights

This is very fast. In fact, we have already calculated it! We accomplished this when we calculated the partial derivatives for the output layer nodes. The gradient of any output layer bias weight is simply Delta$_z$:

$$\delta_z = (z-t)\,z(1-z)$$

Now remember, we calculated two different Delta$_z$'s: one for **node c1**, and one for **node c2**. All we need to do is connect the correct Delta$_z$ with the correct bias weight! Looking at the network layout below, we can see that **bw3** relates to Delta$_z$ for node **c1**, while **bw4** relates to Delta$_z$ for node **c2**.

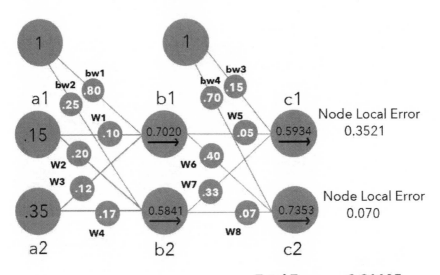

Therefore:

$$\frac{\partial E}{\partial BW_3} = \delta_z = (z-t)\,z(1-z)$$
$$= 0.1432$$

And:

$$\frac{\partial E}{\partial BW_4} = \delta_z = (z\text{-}t)\,z(1 - z)$$
$$= -0.0515$$

Finally! We have now finished calculating the gradients (partial derivatives) for each weight connected to the output layer. Let's move forward and begin calculating the hidden layer weights.

Section 3: Calculating Gradients For Hidden Layer Weights

There are a total of four hidden layer weights situated between the input layer and hidden layer that we will be calculating gradients for. See below.

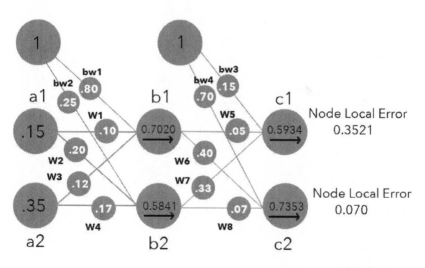

The formula we will use is as follows, with slight adjustments for **w1.** Again, we derived this formula back in Part 2: Stage 3. *Note: we have broken the formula into three parts for easy calculation.*

$$\frac{\partial E}{\partial W_1} = \left(\sum_c \delta_z W_i\right) \text{outb1} (1 - \text{outb1}) \text{outa1}$$

with brace markers labeled ①, ②, ③

Calculating for W1: Part 1

Let's begin by calculating Part 1 of the formula. Note that w_i in the formula stands for an unspecified weight due to the fact we will be dealing with two weights: **w5** and **w6**. If you look at the network layout, you can see that a change in **w1** affects two output layer weights, which are **w5** and **w6**.

There are a total of two output nodes, and therefore we will need to calculate and sum the following.

$\Box_z$ * **w5** for output **node c1**.

Delta$_z$ * **w6** for output **node c2**.

As we discovered when we calculated the gradient for output layer bias weights, we have already calculated Delta$_z$ for each node! A quick review:

For **node c1:**

$$\delta_z = (z\text{-}t)\, z(1 - z)$$
$$= 0.1432$$

Therefore, all we need to do is multiply by **w5**:

$$= 0.1432 * 0.05$$

$$= 0.0072$$

And for **node c2.**

$$\delta_z = (z\text{-}t)\, z(1 - z)$$
$$= -0.0515$$

We multiply our answer by **w6:**

$$= -0.0515 * 0.40$$
$$= -0.0206$$

Now we can implement the summation operator and add the two values together:

$$= 0.0072 + (-0.0206)$$
$$= -0.0134$$

Part 1 of the formula is now complete! Let's plug it into the formula.

$$\frac{\partial E}{\partial W_1} = \overbrace{\Big(-0.0134 \Big)}^{1} \underbrace{out_{b1}\,(1 - out_{b1})}_{2}\, \overset{3}{out_{a1}}$$

Calculating for W1: Parts 2 and 3

Solving for Part 2 is quite straightforward.

The formula is:

$$out_{b1}\,(1 - out_{b1})$$

Substituting our values we get:

$$= 0.7020 * (1 - 0.7020)$$

$$= 0.2092$$

Part 2 is now calculated. If we plug it into the formula, and also plug in Part 3 (which is simply **outa1**), our formula will be finished! *Note that the final answer is very small, and thus we have extended the decimal places.*

$$\frac{\partial E}{\partial W_1} = \left(\overset{\textbf{1}}{-0.0134} \right) \underset{\textbf{2}}{0.2092} \quad \overset{\textbf{3}}{.15}$$

$$= -0.0134 * 0.2092 * .15$$

$$= -0.000420492$$

Calculating for W2: Part 1

Now we will move on and calculate the gradient for **w2.** The formula we will use is below. Again, we will be solving each part in order.

$$\frac{\partial E}{\partial W_2} = \left(\overset{\textbf{1}}{\underset{c}{\sum} \delta_z W_i} \right) \underset{\textbf{2}}{\text{out}_{b2} (1 - \text{out}_{b2})} \overset{\textbf{3}}{\text{out}_{a1}}$$

Calculating for W2: Part 1

Note that w_i in the formula stands for an unspecified weight due to the fact we will be dealing with two weights: **w7** and **w8.** If you look at the network layout, you can see that a change in **w2** affects a total of two output layer weights, which are **w7** and **w8.**

There are a total of two output nodes, and therefore we will need to calculate and sum the following.

$\square_z$ * **w7** for output **node c1**.

Delta_z * **w8** for output **node c2**.

As we discovered before, we have already calculated Delta_z for each node! For **node c1:**

$$\delta_z = (z\text{-}t)\,z(1 - z)$$
$$= 0.1432$$

Therefore, all we need to do is multiply by **w7**:

$$= 0.1432 * 0.33$$

$$= 0.0473$$

And for **node c2.**

$$\delta_z = (z\text{-}t)\,z(1 - z)$$
$$= -0.0515$$

We multiply our answer by **w8:**

$$= -0.0515 * 0.07$$

$$= -0.0036$$

And finally add the two values together:

$$= 0.0473 + (-0.0036)$$

$$= 0.0437$$

Part 1 of the formula is complete. If we plug it into the formula, we have the following:

$$\frac{\partial E}{\partial W_2} = \left(\underbrace{0.0437}_{1} \right) \underbrace{out_{b2}(1 - out_{b2})}_{2} \overset{3}{out_{a1}}$$

Calculating for W2: Parts 2 and 3

Solving for Part 2 is quite straightforward.

The formula is:

$$out_{b2}(1 - out_{b2})$$

Substituting our values we get:

$$= 0.5841 * (1 - 0.5841)$$

$$= 0.2429$$

Part 2 is calculated! Our formula now looks as follows (including part 3, which is simply **out_{a1}**). *Note that the final answer is very small, and thus we have extended the decimal places.*

$$\frac{\partial E}{\partial W_2} = \left(\overset{\textbf{1}}{\overbrace{0.0437}} \right) \underbrace{0.2429 \qquad \overset{\textbf{3}}{\overset{\uparrow}{.15}}}_{\textbf{2}}$$

$$= 0.0437 * 0.2429 * .15$$

$$= 0.00159221$$

Our gradients for **w1** and **w2** are calculated. Now we will quickly calculate the remaining gradients for weights **w3 and w4.**

Calculating for w3
Notice that this calculation is almost identical to **w1.** The only difference is replacing **outa1** with **outa2.**

$$\frac{\partial E}{\partial W_3} = - 0.0134 * 0.2092 * 0.35$$
$$= - 0.000981148$$

Calculating for w4
Notice that this calculation is almost identical to **w2.** The only difference is replacing **outa1** with **outa2.**

$$\frac{\partial E}{\partial W_4} = 0.0437 * 0.2429 * 0.35$$
$$= 0.003715156$$

Section 4: Calculating Gradients For Hidden Layer Bias Weights

Akin to output layer bias weights, this will be fast! The gradient of any hidden layer bias weight is simply the Deltab of the previous layer:

$$\delta_b = \left(\sum_c \delta_z W_i\right) out_i (1 - out_i)$$

❶ All of the letter "i"'s refer to a unique value. This value depends on the gradient we are calculating.

Now remember, we calculated two different Delta_b's for the previous layer: one for **node b1** and one for **node b2**. All we need to do is connect the correct Delta_b with the correct bias weight! This is what the *unique value* is referring to in the formula above. Looking at the network layout below, we can see that **bw1** relates to Delta_b for node **b1**, while **bw2** relates to Delta_b for node **b2**.

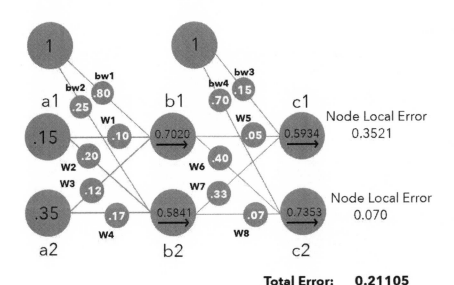

	Node Local Error
c1	0.3521

	Node Local Error
c2	0.070

Total Error: 0.21105

Therefore:

$$\frac{\partial E}{\partial BW_1} = \left(\sum_c \delta_z W_{5+6}\right) out_{b1} (1 - out_{b1})$$

$$= (-0.0134) * 0.7020 (1 - 0.7020)$$

$$= -0.0028$$

You can see above that we have included the actual weights (5 + 6) used to calculate Deltaƅ for **node b1** output. This is simply for clarity.

And:

$$\frac{\partial E}{\partial BW_2} = \left(\sum_c \delta_z W_{7+8}\right) outb2\,(1 - outb2)$$

$$= 0.0437 * 0.5841\,(1\text{-}0.5841)$$

$$= 0.0106$$

Again, we have included the actual weights (7 + 8) used to calculate Deltaƅ for **node b2** output.

Section 5: All Gradients

Calculating the gradients is now complete! Here are all of the gradients we have calculated:

Total Gradients Calculated	
$\dfrac{\partial E}{\partial W_1}$ - 0.000420492	$\dfrac{\partial E}{\partial W_2}$ = 0.00159221
$\dfrac{\partial E}{\partial W_3}$ = - 0.000981148	$\dfrac{\partial E}{\partial W_4}$ = 0.003715156
$\dfrac{\partial E}{\partial W_5}$ = 0.1005	$\dfrac{\partial E}{\partial W_6}$ = - 0.0362
$\dfrac{\partial E}{\partial W_7}$ = 0.0836	$\dfrac{\partial E}{\partial W_8}$ = - 0.0301
$\dfrac{\partial E}{\partial BW_1}$ = - 0.0028	$\dfrac{\partial E}{\partial BW_2}$ = 0.016
$\dfrac{\partial E}{\partial BW_3}$ = 0.1432	$\dfrac{\partial E}{\partial BW_4}$ = - 0.0515

Stage 4: Gradient Checking

After calculating gradients, our next step is to check the gradients. We learned about this in Ch 8. Stage 4: Checking Gradients. Since this step is optional, we will only complete the process for a single weight from our network.

Specifications:
- We will use weight 5 and label it as **w5**.
- We will use 10^{-4} for the Epsilon value.

The general formula for gradient checking is as follows. Note that we have divided it into two parts for easy calculations.

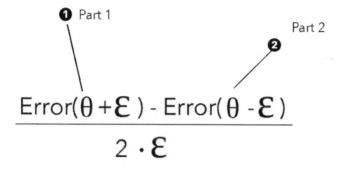

$$\frac{\text{Error}(\theta + \varepsilon) - \text{Error}(\theta - \varepsilon)}{2 \cdot \varepsilon}$$

To compute this we will begin with Part 1 and follow the same 7 steps we outlined in Stage 4.

Part 1:

Step 1. Add Epsilon

To start, we add the Epsilon value to the weight we are checking the gradient for.

$$W5_{new} = W5 + \varepsilon$$
$$= 0.05 + 0.0001$$
$$= 0.0501$$

Step 2. Recalculate the Total Error of the network

Next, we recalculate the total error of the network using the new **w5** value we calculated in Step 1. This means we would work again through Stages 1-2. Note that we did not round any of the new calculations.

This is somewhat challenging to show, but the final result is:

$$\text{Error}(\theta + \mathcal{E}) = \text{Error}(W1, W2, W3, W4, W5 + \mathcal{E})$$
$$= 0.211045192$$

We now have the following part of our formula:

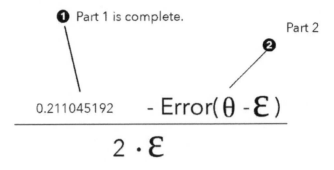

❶ Part 1 is complete.

Part 2

$$\frac{0.211045192 \quad - \text{Error}(\theta - \mathcal{E})}{2 \cdot \mathcal{E}}$$

Part 2

Step 3. Subtract Epsilon

Moving forward, we recalculate the total error again but this time we subtract the Epsilon value from the weight we are concerned with.

$$W5_{new} = W5 - \mathcal{E}$$
$$= 0.05 - 0.0001$$
$$= 0.0499$$

Step 4. Recalculate the Total Error of the network

Finally, we recalculate the total error of the network by using the value we calculated in Step 3. This means we would work again through Stages 1-2.

The final value we arrive at it:

$$\text{Error}(\theta - \mathcal{E}) = \text{Error}(W1, W2, W3, W4, W5 - \mathcal{E})$$
$$= 0.211025091$$

We have now completed the formula:

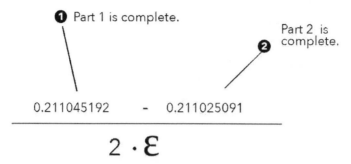

Part 1 is complete.

Part 2 is complete.

$$\frac{0.211045192 - 0.211025091}{2 \cdot \mathcal{E}}$$

Step 5: Calculate the Numerical Approximation

Now that we have our entire formula, we can calculate the numerical approximation for the weight we are concerned with. To do this, the formula that we have completed is worked out.

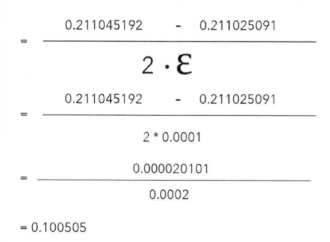

$$= \frac{0.211045192 - 0.211025091}{2 \cdot \mathcal{E}}$$

$$= \frac{0.211045192 - 0.211025091}{2 * 0.0001}$$

$$= \frac{0.000020101}{0.0002}$$

$$= 0.100505$$

Step 6: Measure Against the Analytic Gradient

Next, we check the numerical approximation against the analytical gradient. Doing this will tell us how "far off" the two gradients are from each other. If you recall, the analytical gradient is the original gradient that the network computed.

Difference = Analytical Gradient - Numerical Gradient

$$= 0.1005 - 0.100505$$

$$= -0.000005$$

Then, we convert the value to scientific notation. Note that we are only considering the magnitude of the number, not the fact that it is negative:

Conversion = 5×10^{-6}

Step 7: Compute The Relative Error

The output from Step 6 is 10^{-6}, which is *very small* and difficult to interpret. Is it good? Bad? Ok? To help bring clarity, we will calculate the Relative Error. The Relative Error is calculated by dividing the difference by whichever is larger.

$$= \frac{\text{Analytical Gradient} - \text{Numerical Gradient}}{\max(\text{Analytical Gradient}, \text{Numerical Gradient})}$$

$$= \frac{0.211045192 - 0.211025091}{0.211045192}$$

$$= \frac{0.000020101}{0.211045192}$$

$$= 0.000095245$$

Then, we convert to scientific notation and compare the result to our relative error table:

Conversion = 9.5×10^{-5}

When we look at our table of relative errors, we see the following:

Relative Error	Rules of Thumb
$> 10^{-2}$	High chance the gradient is wrong.
$< 10^{-2}$ and $> 10^{-4}$	A double red flag. Something is wrong.
Between 10^{-5} and 10^{-6}	A single red flag. Use caution.
$<= 10^{-7}$	High chance the gradient is correct.

Therefore, a relative error on the order of 10^{-5} is not bad, although not great, and we should be cautious moving forward.

Stage 5: Updating Weights

It is now time to update the weights! This is the final step in backpropagation, and the last stage in our network. To accomplish this we are going to make use of the general update formula that we covered in Section 2: Stage 5.

This stage is divided into the following sections:
1. Updating General Weights
2. Updating Bias Weights

Updating General Weights

The formula is provided below. We will begin with updating weight **w8**, which you can see within the formula itself. *Note that the update formula does not include momentum. We have omitted this for sake of ease and calculation.*

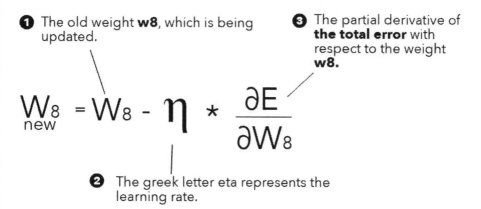

❶ The old weight **w8**, which is being updated.

❸ The partial derivative of **the total error** with respect to the weight **w8.**

$$W_{8\,new} = W_8 - \eta * \frac{\partial E}{\partial W_8}$$

❷ The greek letter eta represents the learning rate.

Let's start!

*Updating Weight **W8***

To update weight **w8,** we will substitute our values into the formula above:

$$W_{8\;new} = 0.07 - 0.5 * (- 0.0301)$$

$$= 0.07 - (-0.01505)$$

$$= 0.0851$$

And that is all there is too it! The new value for **w8** has increased by 0.0126 to 0.0826.

Let's finish this off by calculating the remaining new weights.

*Updating Weight **W7***

$$W_{7\;new} = 0.33 - 0.5 * 0.0836$$

$$= 0.33 - 0.0418$$

$$= 0.2882$$

*Updating Weight **W6***

$$W_{6\;new} = 0.40 - 0.5 * (-0.0362)$$

$$= 0.40 - (-0.0181)$$

$$= 0.4181$$

*Updating Weight **W5***

$$W_{5\;new} = 0.05 - 0.5 * 0.1005$$

$$= 0.05 - 0.05025$$

$$= - 0.00025$$

*Updating Weight **W4***

W_4 new
$$= 0.17 - 0.5 * 0.003715156$$
$$= 0.17 - 0.01857578$$
$$= 0.1514$$

Updating Weight W_3

W_3 new
$$= 0.12 - 0.5 * (-0.000981148)$$
$$= 0.12 - (-0.000490574)$$
$$= 0.1205$$

Updating Weight W_2

W_2 new
$$= 0.20 - 0.5 * (0.00159221)$$
$$= 0.20 - (0.000796105)$$
$$= 0.1992$$

Updating Weight W_1

W_1 new
$$= 0.10 - 0.5 * (-0.0000420492)$$
$$= 0.10 - (-0.000210246)$$
$$= 0.1002$$

Updating Bias Weights

To update the bias weights we apply the exact same formula as above. Let's begin.

*Updating Weight **BW4***

$$BW_{4_{new}} = 0.70 - 0.5 * (-0.0515)$$
$$= 0.70 - (-0.02575)$$
$$= 0.7258$$

*Updating Weight **BW3***

$$BW_{3_{new}} = 0.15 - 0.5 * 0.1432$$
$$= 0.15 - 0.0716$$
$$= 0.0784$$

*Updating Weight **BW2***

$$BW_{2_{new}} = 0.25 - 0.5 * 0.016$$
$$= 0.25 - 0.008$$
$$= 0.242$$

*Updating Weight **BW1***

$$BW_{1_{new}} = 0.80 - 0.5 * (-0.0028)$$
$$= 0.80 - (-0.014)$$
$$= 0.814$$

Wrapping it All up: Final Review

Let's recap what we have accomplished in Part 3.

First, we created a fictitious purpose for our network: classifying two types of images. This (hopefully!) provided a tangible context that we could build our network upon. We then built our network structure, but immediately scaled it down so that it could be effectively used as a training example. Our scaled network included two input nodes, two hidden nodes, and two output nodes.

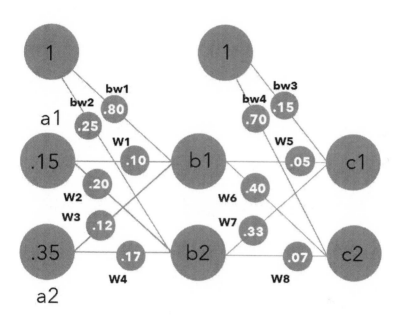

After this we began to pass our chicken image through the network, with the goal of an output of [0, 1].

We used the summation operator and Logistic activation function to pass our information through the network.

$$\sum$$

$$f(x) = \frac{1}{1 + e^{-x}}$$

However, the network output was not [0, 1], but the following:

$$\begin{bmatrix} 0.5934 \\ 0.7353 \end{bmatrix}$$

Next, we calculated the total network error using the SE cost function.

$$SE = \frac{1}{2} \sum_{i = 1}^{n} (t_i - z_i)^2$$

Following this, we began the update process by calculating the error for each weight (which is technically called the gradient, and arrived at by calculating the partial derivative).

We calculated the gradients, and then checked to see if the gradients were accurate using the following formulas.

Gradient Calculation *hidden layer weights.*

$$\frac{\partial E}{\partial W_1} = \left(\sum_c \delta_z W_5\right) \text{outb}_1 (1 - \text{outb}_1)\, \text{outa}_1$$

Gradient Checking Formula

$$\frac{\text{Error}(\theta + \mathcal{E}) - \text{Error}(\theta - \mathcal{E})}{2 \cdot \mathcal{E}}$$

Finally, we arrived at the point of updating the weights. To do this we used the following formula:

$$W_{new} = W_{old} - \eta * \frac{\partial E}{\partial W_{old}}$$

Once we updated the weights, our example concluded. However, in real life the network would continue to loop through Stages 2 - 5 until the network converges when the error rate reaches an acceptable level.

Part 3
Additional Resources

Extended Definitions for Neural Networks

Welcome to our expanded definitions section. In this section we aim to cover core definitions of terms that are often used in neural networks, and have done our best to explain each term in easy to understand language. We have also provided links for further research and examples where appropriate.

Please note that this list is not exhaustive and that all definitions are within the broader context of machine learning and neural networks specifically.

We have organized this section into the following:

1. Terms that are often confusing but describe the same function, action or object. For example, edge and synapse or node and neuron.
2. General definitions associated with neural networks.

Terms That Describe the Same Function, Action or Object

Activation function or transfer function? Node or neuron? Synapse or edge or connection? Which is correct - or are any acceptable? If you have dipped your toes in the world of machine learning, you'll have quickly realized that there is a lack of consistency when it comes to basic terminology used.

To help bring clarity to this, we have put together a list of common terms that are often used interchangeably to refer to the same function, action or object. **Again, please note that all terms are defined within the context of machine learning and neural networks specifically**.

Terms

Activation Function vs Transfer Function = These are the same
*For this guide we have opted to use the term activation function.

Definition: An activation function defines the output of a node given a set of inputs. There are many types of activation functions. The two most common types of activation functions used in neural networks are the Logistic (also called Sigmoid) and Hyperbolic Tangent. Why is this ?

There are two reasons:

1. First, they introduce nonlinearity to a neural network. This is critical because most problems that a NN solves are nonlinear, i.e., they cannot be solved by separating classes with a straight line. The other activation functions in the chart above, such as Step, Sign and Linear, do not introduce nonlinearity.

    2. Second, they limit the output of a node to a certain range. The logistic function produces output between 0 to 1. The Hyperbolic Tangent produces output between -1 to 1.

Also note that Transfer function is sometimes used to denote other aspects of a neural network. See its own definition further down this list for details.

Artificial Neural Network vs Neural Network = These are the same
*For this guide we have opted to use the term neural network.

Definition: Neural Networks (NN) are one type of learning algorithm that is used within machine learning. They are modeled on the human brain and nervous system and the goal of NN's is to process information in a similar way to the human brain. NN's are composed of a large number of highly interconnected processing elements (nodes) working in parallel to solve a specific problem. A key feature of a NN is that it learns by example.

Node vs Neuron = These are the same
*For this guide we have opted to use the term node.

Definition: Inside of an artificial neural network, nodes represent the neurons within a human brain. A neural network consists of multiple layers (input, hidden, and output), and each of these layers consists of either one or multiple nodes. These nodes are all connected and work together to solve a problem.

Synapse vs Edge vs Connection = These are the same
*For this guide we have opted to use the term edge.

Definition: A neural network consists of multiple layers (input, hidden, and output), and each of these layers consists of either one or multiple nodes. These nodes are all connected via edges, which mimic the synapse connections found within the human brain.

Target vs Desired Output Value vs Target Variable vs Ideal Output = These are the same
*For this guide we have opted to use the term target.

Definition: Neural networks are supervised learning algorithms, which means that the network is provided with a training set. This training set provides targets that the network aims to achieve. Technically speaking, the target is the desired output for the given input.

Target is usually denoted as "T" and the input denoted as "X".

Total Error Vs Global Error = These are the same
*For this guide we have opted to use the term total error.

A neural network is successfully trained once it has minimized (to an acceptable level) the difference between its *real* or *actual* output and its *target* output. This difference that the network strives to minimize is technically called an *error* or *total error*.

Additional details: The *total error* is the sum of all *local errors*. A *local error* is the difference that occurs between the *actual* output of a single node and the *target* output that was expected. For example:

      Actual output: 0.75

      Target output: 1.0

      Error: 0.25

If a network has multiple output nodes, the *final local error* is the sum of error of all output nodes, i.e., all *local errors*.

The *total error* is typically calculated using a cost function such as mean square error (MSE) or root mean square (RMS).

Total Net Input Vs Net Input = These are the same

*For this guide we have opted to use the term net input.

Definition: Total input refers to the sum of all inputs into a hidden or output node. It is calculated by adding together the multiplication of each input by its respective weight. This calculation is usually performed using the summation operator. See below.

General Definitions

A short concise definition is first provided for each term, followed by additional details that dive into the nitty-gritty.

Algorithm

An algorithm is a set of instructions designed to perform a specific task.

Additional Details: First and foremost, a NN is an algorithm. More precisely, it is a specific type of machine learning algorithm (along with other algorithms such as random forests, decision trees, nearest neighbors, and many others). Apart from this, algorithms are used *within a NN to* successfully train the network. One of the most common algorithms used to accomplish this task is backpropagation, which makes use of gradient descent to optimize and ultimately train the network.

Artificial Intelligence

Artificial Intelligence (AI) is an area within computer science that aims to develop machines capable of imitating intelligent human behavior.

Additional Details: Neural networks are part of what is called Deep Learning, which is a branch of machine learning. The goal of Deep Learning is to move machine learning towards artificial intelligence. Machine learning is the science of getting computers to act without being explicitly programmed.

Batch Training

Batch training (also called "Full Batch") is a particular form of gradient descent, which is used in conjunction with back propagation to train a network. Stochastic (also called online) and mini-batch training are other popular forms of gradient descent. Each method has its own strengths and shortcomings.

Additional Details: Batch training works by summing the gradients for each training set element and then updating the weights. This updating is technically one iteration. In contrast, online training also updates the weights, but it does so for every training set element - not their sums. This means that online training incorporates many more iterations than batch training.

Chain Rule

The chain rule can be hard to understand. Here are two definitions:

- The chain rule is a way to find a derivative of an equation that is a function found inside another function.

- The chain rule is used to compute the derivative of the composition of two or more functions.

Additional Details: Within a neural network, the chain rule is used to calculate the derivative across an entire neural network. Practically speaking, this makes it possible to adjust the weights and (hopefully) succeed in training the network.

Classification
Classification refers to the sorting, or classifying, of data into groups. For example, a neural network might be presented with a folder of various pictures: some are dogs, others are cats, and others are birds. In this instance, the job of the neural network is to learn how to classify these pictures into three respective groups: dogs, cats, and birds.

Additional Details: Neural networks excel at classification. A fantastic example is Google's Photos app, which is able to organize your photos for you even if you haven't manually tagged them.

Convolutional Neural Network (CNN or ConvNet)
A convolutional neural network (CNN) is a specific type of feedforward neural network. CNN's are typically used with image recognition and in many regards are the core of computer vision systems. However, they are also used in natural language processing.

At a basic level, CNN's have an architecture that is inspired by the animal visual cortex. This architecture naturally lends itself to top-notch performance with image recognition.

Converge
Within machine learning, *converging* refers to the output moving closer and closer to the desired target value. For example, if the desired target value is "1", and the output continually inches closer to 1, it is converging, and if the output were to become "1", it would *converge.*

The opposite of converge is to diverge, which occurs when the output continues to oscillate (undergo fluctuations). In this circumstance, the output is not inching steadily towards the target value, but is fluctuating instead.

Curse of Dimensionality

The curse of dimensionality is a machine learning phrase that refers to the difficulty of working in multiple dimensions.

Additional details: A dimension is an attribute - or several attributes - that describe a property. With neural networks dimensions are the *inputs* to the network.

For example, if an image is broken into pixels and the result fed into a neural network, the number of inputs will equal the number of individual pixels. For a 32x32 image, this would equate to 1,024 inputs - or dimensions.

Herein is where the problem lies: The goal of training a neural network is to find the best combination of weights that yields the lowest error rate - but, the more dimensions that exist, the greater the amount of weight adjustments and combinations *also exist*. With current computing power, the ability to compute *every single combination* soon becomes impossible, even in low-dimensional networks. This problem is what the curse of dimensionality refers to.

To overcome this problem, workarounds - or shortcuts - such as gradient descent are often used.

Dropout

Dropout is a form of regularization that helps a network *generalize* its fittings and increase accuracy. It is often used with deep neural networks to combat overfitting, which it accomplishes by occasionally *switching off* one or more nodes in the network.

A node that is switched off cannot have its weights updated, nor can it affect other nodes. This causes the other weights that are switched on to become *more insensitive* to the weights of other nodes and, eventually, begin to make better decisions on their own.

Deep Learning

Deep Learning is a relatively new field within machine learning that refers to neural networks with multiple hidden layers. The adjective "deep" refers to the amount of hidden layers that exist; the more layers, the "deeper" the learning. The goal of deep learning is to enable machine learning to achieve its goal of creating artificial intelligence.

Epoch

An epoch refers to one forward pass and one backward pass of *all training examples* in a neural network. For example, if you are training a network to recognize images and have a set of 10,000 images, these images are the training examples. An epoch will have occurred once all of the examples are passed through the network. "Passing through the network" includes both a forward and backward pass through the network.

In other words, an epoch describes the number of times a network sees an *entire data set*.

Additional details: Other terms often confused with epoch include batch and iteration.

A *batch* refers to the total number of training examples in both a forward *and* backward pass. For example, 100 images.

An *iteration* refers to the number of times a "batch" of data passes through the network.

Here is an example using all three terms: If you have 500 images (training examples), and your batch size is 100, then it will take 5 iterations to complete 1 epoch.

Gradient

A gradient is the slope of the error function at a specific weight - or in other words, it is the individual error of a single weight in a neural network. Technically it is a vector and arrived at by calculating the derivative of the slope at a specific point.

Additional details: Optimization methods such as gradient descent (see below), calculate the gradients (or errors) of each weight with the aim of minimizing those errors each time they are calculated. This minimization can be viewed as moving down a hill, or descending - and the farther down the hill you go, the less the error is. The ultimate goal is to reduce the *global error* (which is the sum of all local errors) to as minimal as possible.

Gradient Descent

Gradient descent is a popular *optimization* method used to train neural networks, and is commonly used in conjunction with *backpropagation*. *Optimization* refers to minimizing the total error (often called global error) of the network to an acceptable level. The *total error* is often calculated using a method such as Mean Square Error (MSE) or Root Mean Square (RMS).

Hyperparameter

Within machine learning, the term hyperparameter refers to the "knobs" that one can adjust to minimize errors and train a network. Unlike other parameters in a neural network, hyperparameters cannot be learned by the network. In light of this, hyperparameters must be assigned and adjusted manually.

Examples of hyperparameters include:
- Total number of input nodes
- Total number of hidden layers
- Total number of hidden nodes
- Total number of output nodes
- Weight values
- Bias values
- Learning Rate

Additional optional hyperparameters include:
- Learning rate schedule (learning rate decay)
- Momentum (optional)
- Mini-batch size
- Number of training iterations
- Weight decay

Examples of standard model parameters that a network can learn include:
- Weights
- Biases

Learning Rate Schedule

A learning rate schedule allows for the learning rate to be adjusted (usually decreased) while a network is training.

Local Minima

A *local minima* is a false *global minimum*. In other words, it is a false minimal error that neural networks tend to become trapped in and unable to escape. *Momentum* is a popular technique used to help push a network out of it and towards a true *global minimum,* or at least in order to find a local minima that is closer to the true minimum and thus acceptable.

Machine Learning

Machine learning (often abbreviated as ML), is both a field within computer science and also a type of artificial intelligence. At its most basic level, the goal of ML is to create computers that can act *without* being programmed. ML makes use of algorithms to parse (break apart and analyze) data, learn from that data, and then act on that data.

Overfitting

Overfitting occurs when a network performs well with a *specific training set* and minimizes the error, but when presented with a *new* training set the error rate is much larger. For example, say that a neural network successfully trains (minimizes the error) on a data set containing three types of animals: cats, dogs, dogs and birds. However, when a *new* training set of cats, dogs, and birds is introduced to the network, the error is significantly larger.

This often occurs because the network only *appears* to have successfully learned, but in reality has merely "memorized" the initial training set.

On a more technical level, overfitting occurs when a network pays too much attention to unnecessary details called *noise* instead of paying attention to the *signal*.

Parameter

There are two types of parameters within machine learning: model parameters and hyperparameters.

Model parameters can be adjusted by the network itself. In fact, this adjustment is what constitutes the "learning" of a network. Example model parameters include the weights.

Hyperparameter refers to the "knobs" that one can adjust to minimize errors and train a network. Unlike other parameters in a neural network, hyperparameters cannot be learned by the network. In light of this, hyperparameters must be assigned and adjusted manually. Examples include momentum and the learning rate.

Propagation
There are two types of propagation within a neural network: forward propagation and backpropagation. Forward propagation refers to moving data through the network to get output. This output is then compared with the *target* output and any difference is labelled as an error (also called *global error*).

Backpropagation refers to moving *back through the network* and updating the weights. An *optimization* method such as *gradient descent* is often used to do this.

Recurrent Neural Network (RNN)
A recurrent neural network (RNN) is specific type of neural network that contains at least *one feedback connection* - or in other words, a loop. RNN's have shown great promise at learning sequences and performing sequence recognition and association. Applications have included language processing and speech recognition.

There are number of RNN models (architectures), including :
- Fully recurrent network
- Recursive neural network
- Hopfield network

Regularization
Within machine learning, regularization refers to various techniques that are used to prevent overfitting. Penalizing the cost function is a popular technique.

Semi-Supervised Learning
Semi-Supervised learning is one of three types of categories used in machine learning. It is a blend of supervised and unsupervised learning.

Stochastic Gradient Descent (SGD)
Stochastic Gradient Descent (sometimes abbreviated as SGD and/or called *online training or online gradient descent*) is* one of three popular *gradient descent* variants. It is used to optimize a neural network by minimizing the error (also called *global error).* The other popular gradient descent variants are *batch training* and *mini-batch training.*

Additional details: With SGD, the weights in a network are modified after every training set example. What this means is that a *single* training set example is used to update a parameter (weight) in a particular iteration. If a training set is large and has many examples, this can take a long time.

*SGD is technically one type of online training algorithm, but we won't go into the details here. On a high-level, many in the ML field use the terms SGD and *online training* interchangeably.

Supervised Learning

Supervised learning is one of three types of models used in machine learning. In fact, supervised learning algorithms such as neural networks and support vector machines are typically what people think of as artificial intelligence and machine learning.

With supervised learning, the data is a set of training examples with the associated "correct answers". The algorithm learns to predict the correct answer from this training set. An example of this would be learning to predict whether an email is spam if given a million emails, each of which is labeled as "spam" or "not spam".

Classification and regression are two examples of problems often solved using supervised learning.

Additional details: Technically, with supervised learning there is an input (typically denoted as X) and output (often denoted as Y), and an algorithm is used to map the functions from input to output. The input (x) is the training example, the output (Y) is the correct answer, and the algorithm can be any machine learning model, such as a neural network, support vector machine (SVM) or random forest.

Training Set

A training set (also called training data) consists of a set of *training examples*. For example, if you were training a network to analyze handwritten numbers between 1-10, a training example would be a single handwritten digit, such as 9. The training set would be all of the handwritten digits together.

In supervised learning, each *training example* is a pair that consists of an input and output (the "correct answer" of what the input is). The goal of supervised learning is to correctly *map* the input data to the output data, and thus *learn*.

Transfer Function

The term *transfer function* is often applied to different aspects of a neural network. This can make the term incredibly confusing. For sake of clarity, we have opted to not use this term in our book. Possible uses include:

- Referring to the activation function. This is the most common usage for this term, although activation function is the more popular of the pair.
- Referring to the summation function.
- Referring to the summation function and activation function combined.

Unsupervised Learning

Unsupervised learning is one of three types of models used in machine learning. With this type of learning, an algorithm is provided with an input (typically denoted as X), *but no target output* (typically denoted as Y).

Since an unsupervised algorithm does not have any "correct answer" variables (Y) to learn from, it instead tries to find trends in the data. This of course is the exact opposite of how supervised learning works (which is provided with both an input X and target output Y).

Examples of unsupervised learning algorithms involve clustering (grouping similar data points) and anomaly detection (detecting unusual data points in a data set).

Vector

A vector represents a quantity that has two attributes: magnitude (size) and direction. Vectors can be summed and subtracted from one another, and to perform a calculation, vectors are typically broken up in **x** and **y** parts.

Within a neural network, a vector is basically a special type of matrix that has only one column. A vector is an n x 1 matrix, where n represents the number of rows, and 1 represents a single column. Vectors *always* have 1 column in a neural network, and are sometimes referred to as having n-dimensions.

Bibliography

Albright, Dan. "Text Editors vs. IDEs: Which One Is Better For
Programmers?" *MakeUseOf.* N.p., 23 Nov. 2015. Web. 08 Dec.
2016. <http://www.makeuseof.com/tag/text-editors-vs-ides-one-
better-programmers/>.

"Artificial Neural Network." *Wikipedia.* Wikimedia Foundation, n.d. Web.
08 Dec. 2016.
<https://en.wikipedia.org/wiki/Artificial_neural_network>.

"Artificial Neural Networks Technology." University of Toronto, n.d.
Web. 08 Dec. 2016.
<http://www.psych.utoronto.ca/users/reingold/courses/ai/cache/neur
al_ToC.html>.

Bengio, Yoshua. "Practical Recommendations for Gradient-Based
Training of Deep Architectures." *Lecture Notes in Computer Science
Neural Networks: Tricks of the Trade* (2012): 437-78. 16 Sept. 2012.
Web. 5 Jan. 2017.

Bradford, Laurence. "Learn About Text Editors In Five Minutes Or Less."
Learn to Code With Me. N.p., 08 May 2015. Web. 08 Dec. 2016.
<http://learntocodewith.me/programming/basics/text-editors/>.

Britz, Denny. "Deep Learning Glossary." *WildML.* N.p., 28 Jan. 2016.
Web. 08 Dec. 2016. <http://www.wildml.com/deep-learning-
glossary/>.

Brownlee, Jason. "A Tour of Machine Learning Algorithms." *Machine
Learning Mastery.* N.p., 15 Nov. 2016. Web. 9 Dec. 2016.
<http://machinelearningmastery.com/a-tour-of-machine-learning-
algorithms/>.

Bullinaria, John. "Recurrent Neural Networks." *Artificial Neural
Networks* (n.d.): 61-69. 2015. Web. 13 Dec. 2016.

Burch, Carl. "Floating-point Representation." *Toves.* N.p., Sept. 2011.
Web. 03 Mar. 2017. <http://www.toves.org/books/float/>.

"Caffe." *Caffe | Deep Learning Framework.* N.p., n.d. Web. 12 Dec. 2016.
<http://caffe.berkeleyvision.org/>.

Christensson, Per. "The Tech Terms Computer Dictionary." *The Tech
Terms Computer Dictionary.* N.p., n.d. Web. 08 Dec. 2016.
<http://techterms.com/>.

Clabaugh, Caroline, Dave Myszewski, and Jimmy Pang. "Neural

Networks - History." *Neural Networks - History*. Stanford
University, n.d. Web. 08 Dec. 2016.
<http://cs.stanford.edu/people/eroberts/courses/soco/projects/neural-networks/History/history1.html>.

"Convolutional Neural Network." *Wikipedia*. Wikimedia Foundation, n.d.
Web. 09 Dec. 2016.
<https://en.wikipedia.org/wiki/Convolutional_neural_network>.

"CS231n Convolutional Neural Networks for Visual Recognition."
CS231n Convolutional Neural Networks for Visual Recognition.
N.p., n.d. Web. 09 Dec. 2016. <http://cs231n.github.io/neural-networks-1/>.

Dean, Lon. "Artificial Neural Networks Technology." *History of Neural
Networks*. N.p., n.d. Web. 14 Dec. 2016.
<http://www.psych.utoronto.ca/users/reingold/courses/ai/cache/neural4.html>.

Gallagher, Daniel. "Cost Functions in a Neural Network." *Machine
Philosopher*. N.p., 27 Nov. 2016. Web. 19 Dec. 2016.
<http://www.machinephilosopher.com/cost-function-neural-network-intro/>.

Gibson, Chris Nicholson Adam. "DL4J vs. Torch vs. Theano vs. Caffe vs.
TensorFlow." *Deep Learning Comp Sheet: Deeplearning4j vs. Torch
vs. Theano vs. Caffe vs. TensorFlow vs. MxNet vs. CNTK -
Deeplearning4j: Open-source, Distributed Deep Learning for the
JVM*. Skymind, n.d. Web. 12 Dec. 2016.
<https://deeplearning4j.org/compare-dl4j-torch7-pylearn>.

Gorner, Martin. "TensorFlow and Deep Learning, without a PhD."
TensorFlow and Deep Learning, without a PhD. N.p., 6 Feb. 2017.
Web. 03 Mar. 2017.
<https://codelabs.developers.google.com/codelabs/cloud-tensorflow-mnist/index.html?index=..%2F..%2Findex#0>.

"Gradient Checking and Advanced Optimization." *Gradient Checking and
Advanced Optimization - Ufldl*. N.p., n.d. Web. 06 Jan. 2017.
<http://deeplearning.stanford.edu/wiki/index.php/Gradient_checking_and_advanced_optimization>.

"A Hackable Text Editor for the 21st Century." *Atom*. N.p., n.d. Web. 12
Dec. 2016. <https://atom.io/>.

Hamrick, Jessica. "An Introduction to Classes and Inheritance (in
Python)." *An Introduction to Classes and Inheritance (in Python) -
Jessica Hamrick*. N.p., 18 May 2011. Web. 11 Dec. 2016.

<http://www.jesshamrick.com/2011/05/18/an-introduction-to-classes-and-inheritance-in-python/>.

Heaton, Jeffery. *Introduction to the Math of Neural Networks*. N.p.: Heaton Research, 2012. 03 Apr. 2012. Web. 6 Dec. 2016. <https://www.amazon.com/Introduction-Math-Neural-Networks-Heaton-ebook/dp/B00845UQL6/ref=sr_1_1?ie=UTF8&qid=1481043122&sr=8-1&keywords=neural+network+math>.

Honchar, Oleksandr, and Luca Di Persio. "Artificial Neural Networks Approach to the Forecast of Stock Market Price Movements." N.p., Jan. 2016. Web. 15 Feb. 2017. <https://www.researchgate.net/publication/307639575_Artificial_neural_networks_approach_to_the_forecast_of_stock_market_price_movements>.

Hugolarochelle. "Neural Networks [1.1] : Feedforward Neural Network - Artificial Neuron." *YouTube*. YouTube, 16 Nov. 2013. Web. 17 Feb. 2017. <https://www.youtube.com/watch?v=SGZ6BttHMPw&index=1&list=PL6Xpj9I5qXYEcOhn7TqghAJ6NAPrNmUBH>.

Jiaconda. "A Concise History of Neural Networks." *Medium*. N.p., 29 Aug. 2016. Web. 14 Dec. 2016. <https://medium.com/@Jaconda/a-concise-history-of-neural-networks-2070655d3fec#.re2crs5mt>.

Khalid, Muhammad Yasoob Ullah. "20 Python Libraries You Can't Live without." *Python Tips*. N.p., 07 Aug. 2013. Web. 08 Dec. 2016. <https://pythontips.com/2013/07/30/20-python-libraries-you-cant-live-without/>.

Kohavi, Ron, and Foster Provost. "Glossary of Terms." *Glossary of Terms Journal of Machine Learning*. N.p., 1998. Web. 13 Dec. 2016. <http://robotics.stanford.edu/~ronnyk/glossary.html>.

"Library." *What Is Library? Webopedia Definition*. N.p., n.d. Web. 08 Dec. 2016. <http://www.webopedia.com/TERM/L/library.html>.

"Machine Learning." *Wikipedia*. Wikimedia Foundation, n.d. Web. 08 Dec. 2016. <https://en.wikipedia.org/wiki/Machine_learning>.

Marr, Bernard. "A Short History of Machine Learning -- Every Manager Should Read." *Forbes*. Forbes Magazine, 19 Feb. 2016. Web. 08 Dec. 2016. <http://www.forbes.com/sites/bernardmarr/2016/02/19/a-short-history-of-machine-learning-every-manager-should-read/#480b2f8f323f>.

Matthes, Eric. "Python Crash Course." *Python Crash Course by Ehmatthes*. N.p., n.d. Web. 08 Dec. 2016. <https://ehmatthes.github.io/pcc/cheatsheets/README.html>.

Mazur, Matt. "A Step by Step Backpropagation Example." *Matt Mazur*. N.p., 29 Apr. 2016. Web. 20 Dec. 2016. <https://mattmazur.com/2015/03/17/a-step-by-step-backpropagation-example/>.

MIT. "12a: Neural Nets." *YouTube*. YouTube, 20 Apr. 2016. Web. 23 Dec. 2016. <https://www.youtube.com/watch?v=uXt8qF2Zzfo&t=2097s>.

NyKamp, Duane. "Math Insight." *Parameter Definition - Math Insight*. N.p., n.d. Web. 28 Dec. 2016. <http://mathinsight.org/definition/parameter>.

"Python Data Analysis Library¶." *Python Data Analysis Library — Pandas: Python Data Analysis Library*. N.p., n.d. Web. 12 Dec. 2016. <http://pandas.pydata.org/>.

"Python Glossary." *Codecademy*. Codeacadmey, n.d. Web. 08 Dec. 2016. <https://www.codecademy.com/articles/glossary-python>.

Python Programming. Prod. Derek Banas. *YouTube*. N.p., 10 Nov. 2014. Web. 8 Dec. 2016. <https://www.youtube.com/watch?v=N4mEzFDjqtA>.

Rashid, Tariq. *Make Your Own Neural Network*. N.p.: n.p., 2016. 16 Apr. 2016. Web. 6 Dec. 2016. <https://www.amazon.com/Make-Your-Own-Neural-Network-ebook/dp/B01EER4Z4G/ref=pd_sim_351_6?_encoding=UTF8&psc=1&refRID=H3E0YQ1S1E3KMH048PQM>.

Rueckstiess, Thomas. "Welcome to PyBrain." *PyBrain*. N.p., n.d. Web. 12 Dec. 2016. <http://pybrain.org/>.

Ruder, Sebastian. "An Overview of Gradient Descent Optimization Algorithms." *Sebastian Ruder*. N.p., 17 Dec. 2016. Web. 23 Dec. 2016. <http://sebastianruder.com/optimizing-gradient-descent/index.html#gradientdescentvariants>.

Schapire, Rob. "What Is Machine Learning?" *Machine Learning* (2015): 01-16. Princeton University, 4 Feb. 2008. Web. 9 Dec. 2016. <http://www.cs.princeton.edu/courses/archive/spr08/cos511/scribe_notes/0204.pdf>.

"Scikit-learn." *Scikit-learn: Machine Learning in Python — Scikit-learn 0.18.1 Documentation*. N.p., n.d. Web. 12 Dec. 2016. <http://scikit-

learn.org/stable/>.

Sentdex. "Sentdex." *YouTube*. YouTube, n.d. Web. 03 Mar. 2017.
<https://www.youtube.com/channel/UCfzlCWGWYyIQ0aLC5w48g
BQ>.

"Siraj Raval." *YouTube*. YouTube, n.d. Web. 03 Mar. 2017.
<https://www.youtube.com/channel/UCWN3xxRkmTPmbKwht9Fu
E5A>.

"Stack Overflow." *Stack Overflow*. N.p., n.d. Web. 03 Mar. 2017.
<http://stackoverflow.com/>

"TensorFlow Is an Open Source Software Library for Machine
Intelligence." *TensorFlow - an Open Source Software Library for
Machine Intelligence*. N.p., n.d. Web. 12 Dec. 2016.
<https://www.tensorflow.org/>.

"Terminology Used in the Field of Neural Networks." Wiley, n.d. Web. 8
Dec. 2016.
<http://onlinelibrary.wiley.com/store/10.1002/9780470742624.app9/
asset/app9.pdf;jsessionid=34C0345A3FB0A3388EA69CA778C970
3C.f03t04?v=1&t=iwgt2bcl&s=9c127497976d14770e073e156d506
4e997bcd4f8>.

"Torch | Scientific Computing for LuaJIT." *Torch*. N.p., n.d. Web. 12 Dec.
2016. <http://torch.ch/>.

"Unsupervised Feature Learning and Deep Learning Tutorial."
Unsupervised Feature Learning and Deep Learning Tutorial.
Stanford University, n.d. Web. 09 Dec. 2016.
<http://ufldl.stanford.edu/tutorial/supervised/ConvolutionalNeuralN
etwork/>.

"Welcome¶." *Welcome — Theano 0.8.2 Documentation*. N.p., n.d. Web.
12 Dec. 2016. <http://deeplearning.net/software/theano/>.

"What Does "library" Mean in the Case of Programming Languages?"
N.p., n.d. Web. 8 Dec. 2016. <https://www.quora.com/What-does-
library-mean-in-the-case-of-programming-languages.

"Whats the Difference between a Module and a Library in Python?" *Stack
Overflow*. N.p., n.d. Web. 08 Dec. 2016.
<http://stackoverflow.com/questions/19198166/whats-the-
difference-between-a-module-and-a-library-in-python>.

Made in the USA
Middletown, DE
11 August 2018